Shambolic
A Safari Life

Ben Forbes

Copyright © 2023 by Ben Forbes

ISBN: 9798863156545

The right of Ben Forbes to be identified as the Author of the Work has been asserted by him in accordance with the Copyright, Designs and Patents Act 1988.

All rights reserved. No part of this publication may be copied, stored in a retrieval system, or transmitted in any form by any means, electronic, mechanical, recording or otherwise, except brief extracts for the purpose of review, and no part of this publication may be sold or hired, without the written permission of the author.

Cover design by James Shannon.

Interior illustrations by Ben Forbes and DALL·E.

For Botswana's guiding fraternity; you princes
of the Delta, you kings of the Kalahari.

Contents

Introduction
Three Apes and a Screwdriver or How to Build a Safari Camp
Wild Things
Economic Neutrality
Miguel and One-eyed Jack
The Armoured Mongoose
Only Food Runs
Jackson ATC and the Donkey Deceptors
The Guide's Guide to Guides' Exams
The Trouble with George
The Wreck of the Black Crake
Diamonds Aren't Forever
Okavango Crocodile Dundee
The Jao Beauty Pageant
Pirates of the Kalahari
The River Horse
Mugged
The Most Dangerous Thing in Africa
Savuti
The Witch Doctor
Nomad Deluxe
Off the Road
Flotsam and Jetsam and Bliksem
Crap Taxidermy
Bloody Wars, Dread Diseases and Bureaucracy
Last Orders at the Bullet and Bush

Introduction

These stories were originally written down at the turn of the new millennium in a deserted safari camp on Botswana's Linyanti River. My experiences hammered, stream of consciousness, into a dust-clogged laptop with a cracked screen. I was about to be thrown out of the country after almost four years of safari. This collection of tales was the only real trophy I took with me.

Today, most of the safari camps and too many of the people in these stories are gone. The camps either closed or remodelled beyond recognition as fashion dictates. If nothing else, this book is an epitaph to the glory days we shared.

That said, if you sit quietly on the right bend of the Okavango River, you could probably still hear us. Echoes of delirious laughter mingling with the burble of the river, the chuckle of the coucals and the hypnotic bell frogs' chorus.

Tsamaya sentle.

Ben
Gloucestershire
September 2023

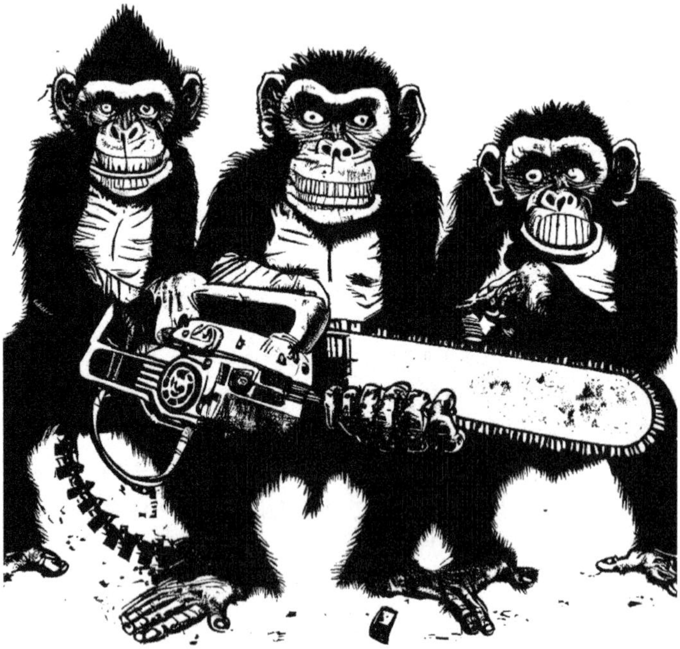

Three Apes and a Screwdriver or How to Build a Safari Camp

A year post-graduation found me wanting something more from life in Europe. Specifically, paid work that was heavy on thrills and light on paperwork.

My first real graduate employment had been in the Hebrides. A place dominated by broad horizons, the turbulent ocean and craggy landscapes. A home for healthy escapism. The reality was vindictive weather and work that trapped me indoors, in an *actual* office. This was like a lobster pot hidden amongst the kelp. One minute you are free as a happy-go-lucky crustacean, the next you are sending faxes to Islamabad and writing reports on gap year candidates. Outside the office, life wasn't much better. Cobain was dead, Brosnan was Bond and O.J. Simpson went psycho. All signs pointed to the exit.

I know now that you can't escape admin. Like an airborne virus, it has drifted into every corner of the planet. History reminds us that the vanguard of every conquering army has been followed by massed ranks of administrators with wax tablets and scrolls. I was hopeful, back in 1995, that I could outrun the laborious, treacly material that clogged the arteries of every workplace I had encountered. It was a naive and ultimately hopeless dream but running felt better than standing to tackle the reality head-on.

So, I was especially receptive to the faint rumours of a wonderful place, a treasure trove of natural delights.

It was Cousin Patrick who threw me an unexpected gift: the rare opportunity to help build a safari camp in northern Botswana. A new camp and a new start. Africa was a dream escape route, a dream so remotely fragile that it could have been shredded by the howling winter gales outside my rain lashed office window. The location of this particular camp was in a private wildlife concession in Botswana's Linyanti region. West of the great elephant herds of the Chobe National Park and north of that wild Eden, the Okavango Delta, amongst ancient ebony, leadwood and marula forest, overlooking a wide lagoon and the river border with Namibia. Slightly to the left of nowhere basically. Africa may lack many things compared to modern Europe, but unpopulated physical space is not one. Botswana is more densely populated by wild creatures than humans. It is a nation overwhelmed by the desiccating power of the Kalahari.

The relatively few people who make a living in the small camps dotted through the country are a diaspora of sorts. They don't share a homeland but a subjective reality with front row seats to the greatest natural show on earth. They get paid cash money to live the wild life, every day of the sun blessed year.

I had carefully prepared for this continental shift by following no discernible career path. First by toiling as the lowest rung on the ladder which emerged from the dark pit of Egypt's refugee management crisis. Then three years studying at the bar, several bars actually, in West London. A euphoric antidote to my reverse culture shock. Eventually emerging with a crushing hangover and a degree in English Literature. Finally, I'd been drawn to the Scottish Islands because they are occasionally magnificent and I like beaches. So, I wasn't obviously qualified for the work on offer in Africa. Nonetheless, like thousands of adventure hungry dreamers before me, I was happy to fake it till I made it.

The job itself was only a temporary post and still one step away from the actual safari business. However, it was a backdoor out of the lobster pot. I resigned from my first real job, sold my VW camper van to cover the flight costs and flew to Johannesburg. When I landed, I had about

£200 left, not even enough to buy a pair of decent binoculars. Forging a good relationship with my potential employer was obviously crucial, first impressions and all that. I expected to deploy some bluff in the interview.

'Have you ever done any large-scale timber construction?'

'I built a dry-stone wall in the Cotswolds once.'

'Great, you are just what we need!'

Interview done, I grabbed a ride north with the Kiwi building contractor, Bruce, and his two top chippies, a pair of Zulu men. On the long drive through the Kalahari they spent most of their time explaining that the Batswana didn't know one end of a screwdriver from the other. Our pair were there to ensure pieces of timber were connected in ways that might support well-fed tourists from distant lands. I wasn't entirely sure, skills wise, what I had to offer but this was all part of my rapidly unfolding master plan to become a safari guide.

Actually, at that embryonic moment, to just become *something* that earned a salary to live in the wild. By the time anyone noticed that I was as gifted with a screwdriver as a gorilla, I'd be in the bush. Closer to the real goal than I had been a month before on the stormbound Isle of Coll.

En route to the site we stopped in Maun, the de facto safari capital of Botswana. Tour operators, air charter companies, hunting outfitters, equipment suppliers and all the associated camp followers vied for space on the dusty roadsides of this outpost town. It reminded me of military supply bases I had grown up on, many moving parts with a single aim to support the front line.

Okavango Wilderness Safaris operated out of a small plot, too small for an almost industry-dominant venture. Assorted four-wheel drive vehicles crammed into a courtyard with a motley collection of offices arranged around the perimeter fence, like a wagon train waiting for a skirmish. This was the outfit whose clients would eventually sleep in the rooms we were going to build. The company had no idea of my construction capabilities, which made two of us. Bruce had people to see, materials to order, staff to locate. I sat out of the way and watched the activity around the yard. I had seen similar set-ups in various parts of the world; just-in-time planning which sometimes works out and, when it fails, creates nothing but glorious opportunity. Learning to appreciate the shambolic as a normal state of things is very liberating, if you can learn to contain your occasional disappointment. The day ended in a local bar where the pulsating chorus of cicadas drowned out the jukebox.

My first Botswana sunrise crept into the sky after a long night practising kung fu on mosquitoes at the staff quarters. The company plot was a collection of bland cement rooms reminiscent of an Egyptian transport jail in which I had once spent a day. Bruce's bakkie was parked outside the wire mesh fence, loaded to the gunnels. I joined the boxes of building equipment in the back of the truck and headed for the real thing. Had I given it some more thought, I would have joined the crew stuffed into the cab with a roof for sun protection and padded seats. Instead, in the fresh early morning with the air filled by exotic bird song, I chose to stretch out in the back with a cigarette. For a start, it smelt a lot less of armpits. Six hours later when we pulled up at the campsite, my knees were burned the colour of overcooked bacon and it was hard to walk. The pain subsided a few days later when the last dermal layer was shed. Maybe it was symbolic, a creature shedding its old skin to inhabit a different version of itself? Or maybe I should have just sat inside with the gang.

Safari camps are like most human creations; they have a shelf life. As the vintage ones rot back into the red earth, new camps emerge like seasonal mushrooms.

The two builders already in camp were an Italian-Maori called Skiv and a South African school-leaver called Tinus, enjoying his first escape from *moeder*. Skiv was the boss on site and, crucially for all of us, this wasn't his first build. Tinus was a pigeon fancier from Welkom in the Free State, a town most famous for its vocal support of the right wing, whites only, Afrikaner Weerstandsbeweging party. If you want some sort of evidence that eugenics are the path to a master race, Tinus was a walking counter-argument. It was clear these two had developed a working relationship of sorts which involved Skiv telling Tinus what to do and Tinus managing to do the opposite. This was nothing to do with a rebellious nature. Rather, it was just an internal programming problem.

Aside from the Zulu master carpenters, there was a local crew of nine. Two were trained builders and the rest had climbed onto the truck either to escape the law or serious alternative employment. Then there was me and I suppose I fell into the latter category. There was going to be a lot of on-the-job training; my dry-stone walling moves weren't going to add much to the project because there wasn't any stone.

It didn't take long to get settled into my new home. There was a multi-purpose clubhouse made from a tarpaulin held up by a tall pole and guy ropes. This covered space housed a collection of battered camping furniture. We had metal packing cases of life-preserving tinned bully beef, rice and that South African wonder relish, *Mrs Ball's Chutney*. I've no idea who this woman was but her creation is a miracle. It turned lukewarm tinned meat products and ant-spotted rice into fine dining. There were beers and cream soda but no fridge, so everything was at room temperature, usually about 32° C. Ablution facilities comprised a row of long drops and a bucket shower with views across the lagoon. The sleeping digs that Skiv, Tinus and I shared were a couple of hiking tents, whilst the crew slept in a massive army tent that had seen a lot of action. Our fresh drinking water came from the nearest operational camp in 200 litre barrels; there was no tap on the base, making it a dip and sip affair. It was also the only place where some of the crew actually washed their hands, so it served a useful dual purpose.

So, what of the work itself? As usual, fact and fiction were poles apart. Building remote safari camps in the African bush was a highly specialised field of work, I thought. Then I had a go at it myself and discovered it was all about Klipdrift brandy, enthusiastic amateurs and power tools. A bit less Frank Lloyd Wright and a bit more Heath Robinson. We split into three teams and started to build the basic structures that would later be adorned with a thatched roof and canvas walls. Lucky tourists would pay over USD 500 a night for the privilege of sleeping in them. If only they knew.

The first stage of a timber stilted room is a series of six-metre gum poles cemented into the ground in a big square, critical to support the planks and teak decking of the floor. These poles look like leafless forests when you walk through them, an eternal autumn. To hide my own complete lack of serious building experience, I encouraged a sense of groupthink in my own team. A few weeks of collective problem solving eventually got me to a place where I could usually build the thing I needed, just once, or maybe twice, to get it really nice. The boss wasn't fooled by any of this; it wasn't causing him to lose any sleep and he needed company more than carpentry.

As the camp started to take shape, our own quarters evolved. A gas fridge arrived to baffle the local hyenas and deny ants access to some of our rations. Mostly, we crammed it full of beer. Then a truck delivered a massive pile of flat packed housing. That was the one and only time it was structurally stable, lying flat in a heap. This pile of cheap pine was going to be the staff village. Each unit came in six parts which you just nailed together; the paperwork called it 'employee housing' but you can find it in DIY stores all over the world, where it is called a garden shed. After a month in the stuffy little tent, I ripped into my fancy new house with enthusiasm and it was upright in no time. My monument to habitational progress had small windows on two sides. If you tried to open them, either the glass or the window frame fell out.

Despite the fact we were now sleeping in Wendy houses, it was pretty advanced stuff for some of the guys who said this was better than their own homes. That early optimism couldn't last. The biggest design flaw in shed-land was a total lack of waterproofing. It was the peak of the rainy season, blisteringly hot days punctuated by dramatic rain showers. The sheds didn't just leak in the frequent thunderstorms of November, they were like sieves. We tried everything from silicon to laminated cardboard to keep the weather out. In very heavy rain, I found that I stayed drier standing outside and holding the door open to allow water to escape. These should have come equipped with flares and lifejackets. Tinus said he couldn't swim.

Between rain showers, we started to build the wash blocks for the new staff village. These converted shipping container units were an improvement on the long drops which had almost claimed several lives. Whilst the deep holes for the septic tanks were being dug, the guys on shovel duty found a human skull. Naturally, this created a fair amount of excitement. As the team excavated deeper, they found human vertebrae and a ribcage. Each time a new body part was unearthed the growing crowd would *ooh* and *aah* before settling back into happy discussion over the find. We were combining osteoarchaeology with our plumbing. Exciting, despite the original plan to literally bury shit in the ground, rather than pull it out.

This person had been buried vertically and, for a while, I was expecting them to discover a bicycle or donkey skeleton beneath him. Sadly, we were denied that entertainment and found nothing more than legs and feet. I know nothing about the rate of human decomposition other than what a prolonged diet of bully beef and fruity chutney can do to the intestines. It looked like the deceased had been planted in the ground for a great many years.

Two cops drove all the way from Kasane, the nearest town, to take the remains away for examination and ask us questions as if it were a red-hot murder enquiry. That is a hard five-hour drive through mud and sand, so it must have been a very slow day in the station house. A bleary-eyed corporal sat down with his notepad and biro; we faced each other in camping chairs for the interview.

'Did anything about the skeleton seem suspicious?'

'Not really, it just looked like a regular skeleton.'

'Where were you when the discovery was made?'

He peered curiously at me, looking for signs that I might crack and admit my part in this vintage crime.

'In my house.'

I pointed at shed No.7 for the sake of clarity and because it was pretty comical that we were even discussing it. The corporal was writing notes and I saw he drew a map of the staff village, although if we were going to be picky about detail, he missed out a lot of the sheds and only included one of the two wash blocks.

'Why do you think this person was buried here?'

Another curious gaze over the top of his limp notebook.

'Hmmm, he must have been dead?'

That finished the interview and Kasane's very own Doctor Watson stood up and wandered back to his colleague who had gathered the bones in a cardboard box. It wasn't a special evidence box, it was from the *Spar* supermarket. As the police bakkie sat idling in the shade of a vast marula tree, we were told to contact them should we find any more remains. Then they were gone, back the way they had come but without their blue lights flashing. If there were any more bodies, they are now underneath the camp's plumbing system.

Despite the obvious logic of building in the dry season, safari tradition dictates that this is rarely done. It is the eleventh bush building commandment, the one after *'Thou shalt not covet thy neighbour's chisel though it may be sharper and newer than thine own...'* As the early rains continued to fall in a near continuous deluge, we were spending increasing amounts of time waiting around for supplies. The supplies were in the back of trucks, buried up to their axles in mud somewhere in the Moremi Game Reserve. Keeping the crew motivated when they lacked the materials to do their work was almost harder than building the camp. You can go fishing with homemade rods and panel pin hooks – you won't catch anything but it passes some time – or you can organise fights.

The guys liked to beat the shit out of each other and pretend they were playing football. Occasionally, someone would actually bring a ball along to these little riots. If we had the time, we would organise games against the neighbouring King's Pool safari camp which was a couple of hours drive away. That way we could export our unique brand of sporting violence whilst appreciating a few of the things that our own team lacked. Personally, that meant enjoying a fully functioning slice of safari luxury. The camp was probably obsolete in terms of progressive safari chic. It was architecturally prosaic, experientially dependable and popular with Americans. Our own mud bath of a construction site was actually the future. Currently though, the future lacked a nice mahogany bar under a cooling thatched roof, so I enjoyed the vintage comforts on offer at King's Pool.

Duma Tau FC were there to covet their opponents' football boots, almost matching strip and a proper pitch with goal posts. King's Pool also had a supporters' club in the form of off duty scullery and laundry staff. These were all things of which our team were keen to relieve them. We were the scrappy outsiders, coming to upset the establishment. What we lacked in ball skills, we made up for in sheer brute muscle and a lack of sporting scruples. Our not very secret weapon was a Zulu colossus called Simon. He had menacing bloodshot eyes, was largely non-verbal and made Idi Amin look like a girl guide. We loved him.

Our biggest problem at these away games was the star player on the King's Pool team. He wore a fancy Liverpool strip and scored five goals to every one of ours. He might have been a chef during the working day but, at the weekend, he was basically *Golden Balls*. The stinging defeat of our previous match was still painfully fresh when I briefed Simon that it would be of great benefit to our side if this *bundu* Pele wasn't playing anymore. I probably should have explained the virtues of tactical subtlety at the same time.

Our assassin took off at a rate of knots, charged across the muddy pitch and bore down on the unsuspecting star. I stood whistling tunelessly on the sidelines and tried to appear nonchalant despite having clearly ordered a hit. Dispensing with any sort of glamour boy fancy footwork, Simon delivered a scything kick that would have split an oak tree, to *bundu* Pele's leg. As the victim with his mangled leg was carried off the field of combat, it was pointed out to us that he hadn't actually been anywhere near the ball at the time. Rather than a sign of sporting contrition, Simon broke into a joyous *Indlamu* dance, honouring his warrior ancestors.

The game was definitely over and we were asked not to return as a sporting team in future.

Wild Things

The best thing about building in the African bush is the wildlife that wanders around the camp scaring the crap out of everyone. If you think sitting in a Land Rover with binoculars is the way to get up close and personal with nature then think again; you need to get out on foot, shake a few bushes and see what falls out.

In addition to the myriad transient species we saw every day drinking at the lagoon, we had a number of semi-resident creatures to keep us on our toes. This included the oldest lion in sub-Saharan Africa, Chester. Anyone who has been close to a male lion when he roars can explain the phenomenal volume of noise generated. He is equipped with a set of lungs that have evolved to function like a foghorn. The ground literally vibrates, hair stands on end; it is brown trousers time. When our ancient king of the jungle roared, we heard the feline equivalent of the rattling hack that typically accompanies aged coal miners – those unlucky folks you see in wheelchairs with an oxygen tank on the back. Each roar terminates in a series of pitiful gasps to replace the expelled air. Chester scared himself more than anything with these vain attempts at liony-ness.

But there was a far more cunning adversary in the form of a cycloptic hyena. One-eyed Jack became a legend in his own lifetime through acts of bravado and perennial oddness. We first met him when our kitchen storeroom was an unloved army tent that smelt like a lot of unfortunate people may have died within its dank, mouldy interior.

It is almost impossible to keep a hyena out of a food tent if he wants to get in. Like the rainwater in our dormitory sheds, it was better to leave the door open and accept the inevitable. Hyenas are equipped with legendary bite capacity, being one of the few creatures in Africa that consider bones to be part of the menu.

The Linyanti night is filled with the soothing music of nocturnal avians and the hypnotic wall of sound generated by reed frogs. Mammals are part of the choir, sporadically declaring either love or territorial rights. At least that should have been what we heard from our bunks in the darkest hours. Instead, it wasn't unusual to be woken from dreams of a nice new chainsaw by the clatter of chairs falling over and plates smashing. That call to arms usually resulted in one or two of us grabbing torches to charge down to the canvas kitchen to rescue our precious rations. One-eyed Jack would casually emerge from the sagging tent like the *Midnight Rambler* with something random between his fearsome jaws, such as a frying pan or a metal coffee pot. It became increasingly obvious that he couldn't care less about the canned goods and bags of rice. I felt pretty sure he was setting up a hardware store under a feverberry tree somewhere, *Jack's General Trading and Scrap Metal*. For a wild beast, he had a singular vision.

Our sleep routines began to alter around these incursions. Shrugging off thin blankets to emerge into the cool of early morning, we took it in turns to search for our big tin tea kettle so we could have a brew.

Ben Forbes

Researchers tend to track animals with GPS collars these days but the quickest way to locate Jack back then was with a metal detector.

After a few weeks of breaking, entering and then just breaking again, Jack began a new routine. He would come and watch us eat supper, loitering with intent at the very edge of the firelight. He had a curious dance, moving his weight from one front foot to the other as if he were standing on hot coals. The endless repetition of this soft-paw shuffle would drive us crazy. He was like a hairy metronome. Invariably someone would crack and chase him off into the night until he ghosted back to the opposite side of the fire to begin dancing again.

It went on for days and then, as we huddled around the bush TV one blustery night, our mono-scopic scrap metal collector was replaced by a much younger hyena, standing in exactly the same spot, staring us out in a direct challenge. This was too much for three humans isolated for months in the remotest corner of a vast wilderness; we charged after him in a show of human solidarity. People always work best together with a common enemy; it's how politics, war and most men function.

A hundred yards into the inky darkness we turned collectively to see Jack with his great unkempt head buried in our curry pot. His single unblinking eye lit brightly by the flames as it watched us, luminous in victory. Outwitted by a hyena! Darwin would have been disgusted. We just tolerated him after that. Months later when the camp finally opened, he graduated from chewing our kitchenware to ripping chunks out of the nice, imported furniture.

These nocturnal antics were a brilliant diversion, but the catalyst that had gathered us there in the first place refused to be side-lined. The camp demanded to be built as quickly as possible with the soft-opening date etched in sales and marketing stone. The rains had put us behind schedule. Tinus was no longer allowed to do anything structural so he was put in charge of collecting firewood and supervising the digging of holes. The crew was supplemented with more casual labourers who did the donkey work, moving timber around the site for the carpenters. Naturally, these new arrivals all claimed to be skilled artisans in the hope that they wouldn't have to lift anything too heavy. As the days ticked through early December, it was often 30°C by midday and lugging 30 kilogram gum poles around all day was like some perverse workout routine.

There were six young men working on concrete production full time but still not supplying enough. Four of them would mix the stuff like a giant dough ball whilst the remaining pair sat and watched. The mixers would grunt and groan, holding their backs theatrically should anyone happen to pass. Then, when the cement was ready, the two wheelbarrow jockeys would take up the huffing chant of the unit to start shifting it around the site. At that stage the mixers would sit right down to happily watch the delivery process before beginning the entire debacle again. It was like watching a tag-team drama society.

Despite all the sound effects, the magic goo still wasn't getting around fast enough for the carpentry teams who were now well-oiled machines. By well-oiled, I mean that Skiv rarely told me to redo the job I had just finished although some of my joinery bordered on the *Kafkaesque*. To ensure supply matched demand, we got hold of a petrol driven concrete mixer. Now we had one guy turning the mixer on, a second throwing in the dry mix and four observers; they truly were casual workers.

We were occasionally required to push the forest back to create ground on which to build. This included the clearing of a densely wooded area for what would become the kitchen. That meant removing all the fallen trees and other obstacles. The largest timber required ten of us to lift it despite trimming as much as we could with a chainsaw. We planned to move it one metre at a time: lift, shift, down, lift, shift, down. A group weights session at the jungle gym. Once everyone was lined up, we made our initial mighty lift. One of the wheelbarrow drivers standing in front of me pointed towards my feet and shouted, 'Snake!'

Now, I couldn't see my feet or the snake because the tree was in the way. There was a general defection of people from around me and I started to struggle with the massive weight of the tree. A tree, I might add, that I now seemed to be carrying single-handed. I couldn't move forwards or backwards because of the snake and I also figured that if I did drop the tree, the final act of this particular reptile would be to fatally bite whoever had dropped a tree on him. It looked like a no-win situation.

So, there I was on a fine Botswana morning, struggling to hold a tree off the ground. A low-rent Hercules entertaining the cowards' collective gathered in front of me to study the most feared of reptiles from a safe distance. They were chatting happily away and pointing like curious window shoppers now that the predicament no longer really affected them.

'What sort of snake is it?' I growled through gritted teeth.

It is worth mentioning that most rural Africans hate snakes above all creatures on God's green earth. Categorisation falls between two groups, 'bad' and 'seriously bad'.

'Black mamba!' yelled one of the cement mixers.

'Eh no! Puff adder! Big puff adder!' argued his neighbour who was peering cautiously around Simon the Zulu's massive shoulder.

'Spitting cobra!' Simon stated with a hint of relish.

This was fast becoming a spectator blood sport. The panel of gleeful nature experts were utterly useless and the fact remained that I was practically balancing on top of my early doom.

'How big is it?'

If they couldn't tell me what type of venom I was facing at least they could describe the size of my nemesis.

'Four feets!'

'Dis big!' The barrow guy held his arms at full stretch and conjured up the snake of his nightmares.

I couldn't hold the dead weight any longer and decided that there was a chance of the snake getting bored and administering a few ankle bites just to liven things up. In a move that pre-dated *Crouching Tiger* by several years, I dropped the timber and simultaneously jumped backwards as far as I could. The twitchy audience scattered at the dramatic manoeuvre. I had only cleared about one metre but nothing had bitten me so it was enough.

Walking around to the other side of the tree, I peered at where I had just been standing, expecting to see an asp of biblical proportions. After a few seconds, the long grass moved slightly to reveal a harmless grass snake which looked like it could have been bested by a well-fed earthworm. It looked even more diminutive when I picked it up, its tiny tongue flickering out and heart thumping in imitation of my own just moments earlier. I waved the featherweight beast at my useless support team who ran yelping into the trees, before releasing him back under the tree so we could do it all again later.

Economic Neutrality

My busy diary was interrupted by a visit to town in an attempt to extend my original three-month visa. I was working on a regular tourist visa just like all the other illegal immigrants on the planet. This was essentially the try-before-you-buy, no promises probationary period. The twilight zone between status and unemployment.

The immigration department had already sprung one surprise visit on us which found me covered in sawdust and sporting a carpenter's utility belt. 'Nothing to see here gentlemen, just another regular tourist going about his usual holiday business!' Tinus was a few metres away standing in a shoulder deep hole which he was trying to measure; he looked so permanently *out to lunch* that they just ignored him. I realised that unless I could gain semi-legal status, even temporarily, my days in paradise were numbered. As entertaining as the day job was, I didn't plan to use up all of my permitted days holding a screaming chainsaw when I could have been pointing a camera at the magnificent wildlife. I also needed to get into some better digs before Jack ate my camera bag.

The office found a couple of empty seats on a flight back into the smoke. Flying out of camp was something of a luxury, especially given the state of the rainy season roads which were littered with bogged four-wheel drive vehicles. The tough little Cessna aeroplanes that hauled humans around the Okavango were the vital support act to the safari industry. The pilots, with characteristic sardonic wit, liked to describe tourists as self-loading cargo. In reality all of us were crammed inside the same noisy little cabin watching as small screws vibrated out of the plastic lining. The only significant difference was that the folks in the back could afford the aviation fuel. The real luxury of travelling by light aircraft was outside the scratched perspex window, the elevated views of the unconquered wilds of northern Botswana.

We landed in Maun late on a Sunday afternoon with a purple dusk fast approaching. It was odd to be standing on smooth cement after months of dirt in varying incarnations. Once I had helped roll the Cessna into a line of similar light aircraft, the pilot grabbed a number of canvas mailbags and hustled for the service exit in the chain-mesh fence. Clearly, he had something to do with his evening which left me, my muddy duffel bag and many hours to kill before the government offices would open the following morning. The little aircraft ticked and crackled beside me as the metal began to cool over its airframe, the entire place was going to sleep and I was alone. I say alone, but actually Tinus was with me, en route to South Africa to check on his beloved racing pigeons.

It was only my second visit to Maun. The company office was closed, I didn't know how to reach the company housing plot and I wasn't prepared to spend money on a hotel room. Truthfully, I didn't actually have any money. I'd sold a classic VW camper, my only cash-convertible asset, to buy my open return air ticket to Johannesburg. I suppose you could say I was economically neutral, like those German craftsmen, *wandergeselle*, who travel the planet trading skills for room and board.

'I'm going to my uncle's house,' explained Tinus and he pointed for the sake of clarity, 'it's over there.'

I had exactly no alternatives so I accepted what sounded like an offer of a bed for the night. With hindsight, I should have just slept on the ground next to the airport terminal.

'Lead on Macduff!'

Tinus looked puzzled but said nothing. Maun is built along a stretch of tar road with scores of dirt tracks sprawling in every direction. Tinus explained that his uncle was involved in road building. As we walked, the quality of the buildings diminished. *Tinus Tours* didn't give much away; several times the guide slowed to a stop in front of a likely building, only to heave his bag back onto his shoulder and trudge onwards. We had walked for half an hour, past increasingly sorry looking houses, in increasingly thick sand when we arrived at *Chez Blacktop*.

The house had an industrial air about it, like a skip with doors. The front of the building was covered almost entirely with an aviary, the occupants of which became crazed as we approached. A living, many-feathered doorbell and intruder alarm all rolled into one.

Before we reached it, the front door was opened by a woman who matched the property. She had seen better days.

'Hello, Tinus,' she said without much enthusiasm.

'Hello, Aunty,' he replied.

We definitely had the right address. She peered suspiciously at me over her nephew's left shoulder. As Tinus hadn't bothered to introduce me, she may have thought I was just a stalker, trailing her relative silently in the soft sand. Before she shouted a warning, 'Look out Tinus, he's behind you!' I took the opportunity to introduce myself.

'Hello, I'm Ben. Tinus said you might be able to put me up for the night?'

The lady of the house gave this a bit of thought before venturing, 'I'm his aunty. you know!'

'Right,' I said, considering the long walk back into town to find a cheap hotel before it became totally dark.

That internal debate was interrupted by our hostess who ushered us into the house which had a certain pet shop aroma to it. The air was definitely fresher outside next to the cramped birds.

'You can sleep right here,' explained aunty, pointing to an army camp bed which for some reason was in the front hall. 'Everyone's in bed. There might be food in the fridge.'

That was the last I saw of her that day as she disappeared to the back of the property. Tinus went straight to the fridge and pulled out a plate of something which looked like it should have been in the aviary outside. I left him to his micro fried chick-something and lay down on the cot where I was lulled to sleep by the sticky heat of the night.

Morning broke to the high-pitched chirping of several hundred captive avians close to my head. Opening my eyes, I saw a man standing in the kitchen doorway, regarding me with a glazed expression on his weathered face. That was fairly convincing evidence that he was probably related to Tinus, no stranger to bemusement himself. It occurred to me that in all the late-night excitement, aunty had neglected to explain there was a stranger sleeping in the hallway. I gave him a quick explanation of how this had come to pass which seemed to remove any concerns he might have had.

'I'm Tinus' uncle,' he replied. 'It's breakfast out there.'

Uncle pointed to the front door before heading back the way he had come.

As I had slept in my clothes, it didn't take me long to get ready. I washed my face and brushed my teeth at the kitchen sink. There was a clock on the wall which said half past seven, the immigration office opened at nine, it was almost time to start walking.

Stepping outside, I could see that the family was having a braai in the front yard. Tinus emerged from the aviary with a handful of chicks.

'These ones won't live,' he explained as he casually broke their necks with his thumb. I'm no expert on the handling of delicate birds and I don't think Tinus was either. Uncle was watching without concern for either the chicks or his nephew's sanity; he was drinking a beer.

The braai itself was a very rusty repurposed two hundred litre diesel drum with ventilation holes drilled unevenly around the base. It had a large square of fencing wire mesh as a surrogate grill.

'I made it myself,' said Uncle, in a tone of voice closer to shame than pride. I had decided that I should make my excuses and leave as soon as possible. Rather leave the family to catch-up on personal matters without an uninvited party crasher to feed.

'Do you want to see the monkey?'

Aunty had appeared and, in the cruel light of day, she looked even more shrunken by the hardships of her environment.

'Sure.'

It would have seemed rude to turn her unexpected offer down so I followed her around the side of the house. Continuing the theme of captive wildlife, an old vervet monkey was caged behind the building. He looked as if he had spent too much time humouring his captors and was now just biding his time.

'That one in there look!' for the sake of clarity, Aunty pointed at the only monkey in the near vicinity before continuing, 'we called it monkey.'

The aged simian hung his head in disbelief and groaned at the tragedy of it all.

'Well, thanks very much for the bed, Tinus' aunty,' I said, backing slowly into the house to collect my bag from the hall, 'I'll find my own way out.'

'I haven't had breakfast yet,' said Aunty to the monkey.

I went out the front door, Tinus was flipping the now limp chicks into the embers of the braai. Who knows, maybe they *were* the braai? Uncle had collapsed sideways in his camping chair suggesting that maybe it wasn't his first beer of the day. My escape from the lunatic asylum went undetected. I'm sure the monkey could have gotten himself out if he really wanted to.

By mid-morning I had extended my visa, just another tourist who couldn't bear separation from the Eden he had stumbled upon, and I was soon in a Cessna back to camp. I doubt anyone at immigration was fooled. Most real tourists have clean clothes and don't carry their possessions in a sun-bleached canvas bag that was clearly made locally. Either way, that was enough of Maun for another few months.

The entire surreal visit could have been a dream except for the pet shop smell that lingered on my clothes. Skiv was ecstatic to see that Tinus hadn't come back with me and we took the rest of the day off to celebrate. We only finished celebrating when we managed to drive Skiv's Toyota Hilux into the Linyanti River. As rite of passage experiences go, Tinus could return home with a clean bill of health and good conscience. He had achieved plenty of exercise, hadn't picked up any bad habits he didn't already possess or any misspelt tattoos.

By European gap year standards, it would be deemed an abject failure.

Miguel and One-eyed Jack

In terms of construction, we had caught up with all the timber work the rains had delayed and additional talents were needed on site. There was a plumber pacing out his trenches and filling them with lengths of fifty-millimetre pipe to carry fresh water in and a hundred- and ten-millimetre pipe to encourage sewage to depart. It wasn't difficult and we all had a crack at connecting pipes and measuring angles of drain. We also discovered that you could use the pipes as a communication system of sorts, it was at least as effective as the High Frequency radio. You could just chat to a mate further down the line or use them to deliver disembodied mutterings to unsuspecting people. A favourite was to ambush wheelbarrow pushers by barking, 'Faster! Faster!' and cackling as they jumped in the air before heading off down the path like the roadrunner.

We were good at livening up our days.

The brickwork was something else though and the owner of the concession was very particular about it. He sent his own man all the way from Johannesburg, an ancient Spaniard called Miguel who led a team of three tiling experts. He claimed to be in his sixties but looked about eighty; either way I thought he should be retired. Miguel spoke in a peculiar gringo-speak of his own devising which meant that the Batswana had no idea what he was talking about most of the time. Neither did I. He was a true master of the ambiguous question and would say things like, 'You know 'im that one?' It was like a word association game where you had to guess if the person in question lived in the camp, in Botswana or even in Africa for that matter. Then you spent the next half an hour trying to narrow the options down from millions to hundreds. Usually, we never could fathom out who Miguel was referring to and it didn't seem to bother him as he sat shaking his head and saying, 'He's a good one, that one!'

Miguel claimed to be a devout Roman Catholic despite keeping a well-thumbed copy of *Hustler* and a bottle of his special wine in his quarters. These were his illustrated scripture and blood of Christ. He would sit in the late afternoon on the steps of his cabin, muttering to himself whilst studying the magazine like it was some ancient scroll filled with revelations. Occasionally, he would discover something particularly offensive to his religious sensibilities and utter the stock phrase, 'Bloody bastard that one!' He always looked extremely happy on these sin-searching missions.

Miguel, being a proud city-born Spaniard, hated the bush with a vengeance and had nothing good to say about the remarkable wilderness all around him. His skills were typically deployed in the safe surroundings offered by luxury homes in Sandton and Bryanston. He had arrived in camp with a case of his own special sweet wine which we administered to him each night as a pacifying agent. He complained that his liver was no good anymore and drank until he was rambling away in slurred Spanish. This was the only way he could face another night in the wild. When we talked about lions and other night visitors around the campfire, Miguel would cross himself and reach for the holy water.

Not long into his stay with us, he had a run in with that nocturnal curiosity, One-eyed Jack. Miguel went looking for his wine in the storage tent and Jack was borrowing one of our saucepans. They met in the doorway. We heard a howl from the Spaniard and Jack dropped his swag in fright.

'Shit! Big one!' yelled Miguel as he collapsed into a bush holding his petrified liver.

It took a bottle and a half of wine to get him to sleep that night and the following day his crew worked double time to complete the job and get home to safety. Two days later they had finished and Miguel was packing his bag before the last tile was in place. He insisted that we drive to the airstrip hours before the flight was due to arrive and sat rigid in the truck cab, windows wound up to keep nature from creeping in beside him. The tiler kissed the fuselage of the aircraft that had come to rescue him and hugged the bemused pilot before clambering in and slamming the door behind him.

The Armoured Mongoose

One week post-Miguel, the almost-complete camp was polished up for the opening ceremony. An event which would be attended by some company staff, Botswana's vice-president and various important persons from the Wildlife Department. The property was officially named *Dumatau*, Setswana for *The Place of the Roaring Lion*. We did the industrial version of children cleaning their bedrooms, shoving loose items behind any available cover or under tarpaulins which we hoped nobody would bother to investigate.

The convoy of company Land Rovers arrived and began to disgorge drunken dignitaries. The pilots swore that they had all departed from Maun in good order, so how they had become inebriated between the airstrip and camp was a mystery.

I kept a very low profile which was what the office staff wanted; after all, builders build, they don't schmooze. One highly vocal accountant from town was trying to explain the camp layout to a wildly swaying big shot from the Land Board. The real estate expert pointed at the kitchen storeroom and explained that it was a manager's house while his audience grasped the trunk of a palm tree to remain upright. At the pool, which was empty because we still had to fibreglass a crack in the bottom, one of the office team was trying to get undressed. She was either so drunk that she couldn't see the pool was dry or she was sober and couldn't swim. The vice-president and his close entourage remained professional though, looking politely interested in things that probably didn't interest them at all.

Skiv and I liberated a case of fine imported beer and retreated from the party. We didn't break cover until we heard the convoy heading back to the airstrip in the late afternoon.

Once the public relations exercise had been concluded, Dumatau Camp officially opened to paying punters. Shortly after that, we actually finished building the camp. This meant that the construction crew who had been living in each other's pockets for months were loaded onto a truck bound for Maun and either the bank or the bottle shop to deposit their earnings. Skiv loaded his gear into the back of the *Bush Bitch*, as his Hilux was known, and headed for a camp on the southern edge of the Okavango.

We had both been cramming for the national guides' licence exam, which only happens a couple of times a year. Skiv had landed a guiding job and wasn't especially sad to be packing the tools away for a privileged life cruising around watching nature in all her majesty. If there was a better way to earn a living, neither of us could imagine it.

I stayed on at the newly opened camp as a short-term maintenance solution and started to take on some hosting responsibility. Superficially that meant my wardrobe expanded to include a couple of uniform shirts and a fresh set of khakis. In reality, I had more knowledge of the game drive routes and local wildlife hotspots than the incoming guides who hadn't seen the area before. I just lacked the correct paperwork to take guests out on drives and walks; my trusty *Blue Peter* badge didn't seem to cut the mustard on that front, which was a major disappointment. Regardless, I knew a regular guiding position would come my way sooner or later, it was just a case of making myself useful in the meantime.

I achieved this by waiting for that most sacred hour, the post-lunch siesta, when all of Africa dozes in the shade, to start my chainsaw and try to wrap up a few loose ends back of house. The point of this anti-social exercise was to elicit a predictably angry response from the camp manager who immediately banned me from construction work unless all the guests were out of camp. I never lifted a power tool in anger again, job done.

I was able to turn my creative skills to smaller tasks and none was more pressing than the suit of armour I was shaping for the smallest member of the Dumatau team. Now that we had an office, it was occupied by a number of young women who kept the camp running whilst the guides were out hunting down tip-inducing wildlife.

One of the girls had adopted a stray banded mongoose, nicknamed *Igundane* from the isiZulu word for rat. I had been a voice of reason and said that from my short experience at the camp, every single wild thing we tried to adopt or pet name had ended up dead. It was like an instant curse. The girls were having none of it and I had to admit Igundane looked very funny toddling up and down the pathways close to the office which housed his cardboard box palace.

Abandoned too young to learn the rules of survival, our slender pal spent all his time staring at the ground looking for snacks. An amateur's mistake because, in Africa, death often comes from above. I gave him a couple of lessons, pointing into the blue sky and flapping my arms like a bird of prey. He sat bemused but entertained during these sessions before wandering off with his snout twitching millimetres from the ground. Hopeless.

The only viable solution was to protect him from himself and the feathered assassins wheeling in the thermals above camp. I shaped a small, segmented carapace from a Castle Lager can. He looked like a Roman legionnaire on patrol. Surprisingly, Igundane didn't resist his new coat of arms which was held in place by two thick rubber bands under his smooth belly. Staff and guests alike loved it when the beer tank ambled past them and I wondered if, maybe, our latest pet had a brighter future than his predecessors.

One incredibly warm morning I was helping the concession mechanic to change the filters and oils in our generator. He was a fractious Englishman and I tended to introduce him as a mechanic to which he always replied in a threatening grumble, 'Land Rover Engineer!' Like that made the slightest bit of difference to anything. Anyway, we got the job finished, ran a system check and walked back up to the workshops on a path that passed the office and kitchens.

'Christ you've got some good birding here!' said the grease monkey which prompted me to look up and see that we had close to fifteen raptors circling in a thermal directly above us. A couple of yellow billed kites had dropped to just above tree level and I had a sudden sense of doom.

Jogging the few metres to the office I looked in the mongoose palace, it was empty. I looked up at the hook we kept his body armour on and it was there. This was bad. His favourite morning walk was the path down to the big boma where the barman usually found some unloved bar snacks to give him.

It wasn't far before I found him, his soft fur matted with blood and a great tear along his flank. I hoped it had been quick and I was surprised there was so much of him left to bury; usually a raptor just disappears with his kill to a quiet roost.

Naturally, there were tears and outrage when the news spread. The screw loose camp hand offered to blast any kite he saw with red on its bill to smithereens. The brief burial ceremony put most of these emotions to rest. We kept the beer can armour as a reminder of happier times.

Only Food Runs

The first guests into camp were all travel agents, invited to experience our wonderful new property. This is the primary perk of working on the safari sales front. Just like government officials, you give them plenty of alcohol to smooth over the rough edges found in any newly finished camp. They get to see a great new property, we receive some direct feedback for our snag list and everyone is happy.

Their first afternoon in camp was livened up by a couple of bull elephants redesigning our pathway railings. I would have enjoyed it more if I hadn't just put those same rails up a week ago. Still, you can't start shooting naughty elephants in front of guests, can you?

The day ended with a lovely candle lit dinner around the great dining table, eating off brand new crockery served by staff resplendent in crisp new uniforms. Brandi, the Californian travel agent staying in the most distant room, wanted to get an early night and one of my duties was to walk guests home after dark. As we walked, we discussed the merits of unfenced camps and I delivered the company spiel on an authentic wilderness experience. It had truly amazed me to learn that some people did build fences around their camps, further insulating their guests from what they had come to see. There was none of that in our outpost which was part of its attraction.

The narrow pathway flowed around a towering termite mound. As we passed this landmark, something started moving loudly towards us from the thick bushes that bordered the sandy trail. It sounded a lot like someone dragging a sack of potatoes or a corpse. Before my companion had a chance to ask my opinion on all of this, both our curiosities were answered.

The undergrowth parted six metres away to reveal an adult lioness with a recently killed impala ewe in her jaws. Now, if you are going to meet a wild animal jealously guarding their precious food supply, you might prefer something like a squirrel grasping a nut. I know that is what I would have preferred at that late hour anyway. I wasn't exactly sure what the cat thought about it all. She dropped her kill, flicking her tail the way felines do when they want to play. Grizabella already had her supper, we just needed to make sure she understood that we didn't want to take it off her.

'Walk back to the corner so you are out of sight,' I muttered to the agent who was holding her breath. 'I'll stay here and keep my torch on her.'

She didn't bother to reply but I could hear her shuffling backwards. The lioness lowered herself a bit and tried to penetrate the beam of light, looking for the source of the sound. It suddenly occurred to me that I should have cautioned Brandi not to run. Only food runs. Running can trigger a game of chase and big cats are excellent at that. I turned to offer this gem of wisdom and saw the beam of her torch pumping up and down as she headed back to the bar. Her retreat remains an unbroken sprint record on that pathway.

Fortunately, the lioness was fast losing interest as I backed further away to the termite mound. To my relief, she picked up her trophy and headed back into the bush. I loitered quietly in the darkness for a few moments to check that she was still heading away before I started back to the main *lapa*. By the time I arrived, Brandi was on her second double whisky and part way through one of three cigarettes she had smouldering in an ashtray. The rest of the group were crowded around her and, not wanting to feel left out, they recounted similar stories that they made up on the spot.

'Hell, at least we know there are lions here now!' a fellow agent summed up the general opinion.

'What a story to tell your clients!' She liked that and the terror was eased by the fact that she had a *bona fide* bush tale to share. A tale worthy of the campfire debating society in any safari camp.

I ended up driving Brandi back to her room as the Dutch courage and post-adrenaline slump were weighing heavily on her legs. She asked me to turn on all the lights and check the tent before she would walk inside. There were no cunning predators curled up on the bed, just a towel in the shape of a benign crane. Brandi skipped the next day's game drives in favour of the bar and swimming pool. I heard that, at the following camp on their itinerary, an elephant did some panel beating on the vehicle she was in. We just hoped our animal magnet would make it home alive otherwise all of this outstanding PR was going to be wasted.

God knows how the wildlife entertained itself during slow evenings before the arrival of the eco-tourist?

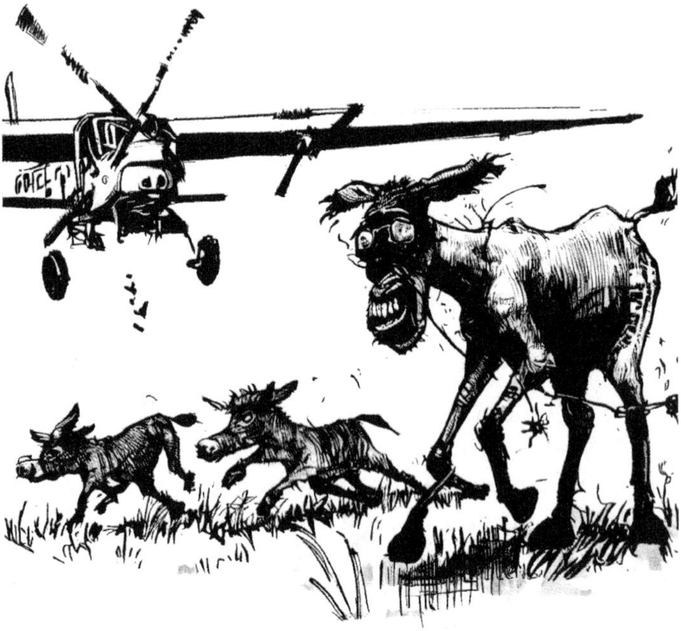

Jackson ATC and the Donkey Deceptors

It may sound like a post-punk band but actually they were the first people any guest arriving at Jedibe Island Camp met. Jedibe was built on a beautiful island deep in the heart of the Okavango Delta. Surrounded by papyrus fringed waterways that led to glorious lagoons, scattered islands and eventually the main Okavango River channel. The only thing the camp lacked was enough room for an airstrip and so the neighbouring island had become the default flight deck. There was a small community of fishermen and their families living there. In the past it had been a leper colony and very occasionally you might see an aged African suffering from that dread disease. This interesting local history wasn't typically shared with guests.

    A crucial role at any bush airstrip is to make sure the ground is clear of obstacles, ideally before the aircraft lands. Pilots become quite agitated when they discover a giraffe or small herd of elephants in direct line with their propellor. Luckily for the aviators, the island was surrounded by miles of swamp so it was rare for any mega fauna to make an appearance. What it did have though were donkeys, that staple resident of all African villages. Beasts of burden and notorious traffic botherers.

    Our solution was to employ both an airport manager, the formidable Jackson of *Air Traffic Control* and two donkey deceptors. Jackson had

Shambolic

taken a piece of planking to create Terminal Three, a short bench with no facilities. People always asked where Terminals One and Two were but Jackson never told them. The role of airport manager had been decided by committee in the village. I suspect that Jackson either had some dirt on the committee members or just offered to fight any man wanting the position. He took his job seriously and wore an old uniform shirt cast-off by someone in camp, army trousers and standard issue army boots. On his chest he wore a name badge that we had ordered from Maun, a nice piece of tin stamped with Jackson ATC. Next to that he proudly wore his ZCC star to show his obedience to the Zion Christian Church, although some sceptical observers called it the *Zulu Crime Club*.

There were various perks to being ATC. It gave Jackson access to the camp for a start, more specifically the first aid kit and assistance from the manager, Gypsy, who functioned as the local medic. That is quite an employee perk when you consider the only alternative is to risk your life on the hospital boat that speeds between remote villages and the basic hospital in Shakawe. That boat caused more accidents than anything else afloat on the river. The helmsman was a complete lunatic, believing he had some divine protection because of the large red cross painted on the cabin roof. The number of times he almost sank made it seem more of a target than a talisman. Jackson was also a frequent visitor to our small workshop where we would repair whatever he had dragged in – a ruined outboard propeller, a hole in his leaky mokoro or re-soldering snapped wires together in his precious radio.

What I loved most about my time with Jackson was his enthusiastic, carefree method of loading and unloading client luggage. The little Cessnas lacked storage space, just a very small area behind the last row of seats and a pod riveted onto the bottom of the fuselage.

The air charter companies were very clear about weight allowances and types of luggage but guests would often hardly give these a passing thought. They would stand in the dazzling sunshine and gape open mouthed as Jackson tore into their precious belongings. Rigid suitcases don't fit into small aircraft as well as nice soft duffel bags, the company guidelines advised. Jackson was the instant karma offered to anyone who had ignored the advice and thought they had gotten away with it. Handles were torn from cases, shiny plastic shells were scraped out of the tight opening to the pod. Long shoulder straps usually ended up in two halves, but that wasn't the best part. When it was a re-loading exercise and it became obvious the first-world freight wouldn't fit into the small cavity between the landing gear, Jackson deployed those size 12 army boots. He would stamp and kick with all his considerable strength, the luggage would creak, crack and sometimes just splinter under the vicious attack. I never saw a piece of luggage that he couldn't break and all undertaken with a look of sheer joy on his typically calm face.

The guests wouldn't say a thing, that was part of the fun really. Would you start an argument with a giant of a man clearly relishing his role in redesigning your Louis Vuitton wheelie bag? The pilots fought to keep a straight face but given their hatred of the entire baggage problem they sweated over daily, it was really quite a treat. When he had finished beating the bags into submission, Jackson would straighten up, offer a brisk salute and announce, 'Jackson ATC, mission complete!' before handing over a collection of handles to the bemused owners.

At a busy airport like ours, which might have to handle one light aircraft every couple of days, Jackson asserted that he should have some ground crew. That is how Jedibe Terminal Three gained the Donkey Deceptors, a pair of young relatives that Jackson cunningly nudged onto the payroll. The job description was pretty simple: when you hear the drone of an approaching aircraft, make sure the airstrip is clear of mobile obstacles. The number one danger being Jedibe's small population of donkeys.

In Botswana, most donkeys are hobbled to prevent any thoughts of escape to a better life but this wasn't necessary on an island surrounded by crocodile infested swamps. The Jedibe donkeys could roam free, at least around their small domain which included the airstrip. The Deceptors would charge up and down the rutted runway, donkeys would flee in all directions and usually end up back in the forbidden zone. Considering the narrow requirements of the job, the Deceptors never really developed an effective system but Jackson didn't mind. He sat in the shade and barked commands until the pilot blasted through the middle of the mayhem and rolled to a stop beside the bench. I think

Shambolic

it amused him that anyone capable of flying a plane couldn't handle a couple of suicidal donkeys.

I was in the camp office one morning when Jackson made a sudden appearance. Never one for beating around the bush, he announced that he had a problem with his *Ntondo* and promptly dropped his shorts. It might be worth mentioning that I wasn't alone in the office, there were also two laundry ladies and the manager, Gypsy. Everyone stared in varying degrees of disgusted curiosity at the sorry state of Jackson's appendage. The laundry ladies backed away for fear of catching anything, whilst Gypsy and I leant in to marvel at the hideous affliction. A dire disease straight from the Middle Ages or the hut of the least hygienic girl in the village.

'I hope you don't go near your wife with that thing?' was the first semi-medical suggestion I could think of.

There was nothing in the camp medical kit that was going to be of any use apart from a plaster he could apply if the thing fell off. Gypsy told him to zip it back up and we handed over some painkillers and ointment that were going to do almost nothing to cure whatever the hell he had contracted.

Eventually, Jackson was forced to join the other unfortunates on the hospital boat. He came back from Shakawe a new man, as he proudly showed us on arrival. There are few things less welcome in a safari camp than rampaging STDs, but one of those things is a visit from the airport inspectors.

Every camp manager is responsible for maintaining their airstrip to certain minimum standards. Every inspector is responsible for trying to close down those same airstrips for transgressions of obscure regulations. Like most tax-payer funded outfits, they are a league of extraordinary bullshitters. The Jedibe airstrip was infamous throughout the Delta for being a bit of a white knuckle special. It was somewhat crooked, it developed potholes as fast as Jackson's *Ntondo* did and when it rained it just turned into a lagoon.

A brief letter arrived to inform us that an inspection team was heading our way. In preparation, I dug out the report from the previous visit which was all good news. We had failed that one and the strip had been closed until we put white markers along the edges of the designated strip. This was despite the fact that no pilot had ever failed to differentiate between airstrip and swamp. Although one overloaded aviator had once overshot and ended up in the lagoon but that was mostly human error.

Inspection day arrived. Jackson and I stood listening to the unmistakable drone of a Cessna from across the sea of papyrus. The pilot made a couple of low passes over the island before dropping into a shallow turn and bouncing down the strip. It was a landing that proclaimed the poor quality of the runway. A practical demonstration of how not to build an airstrip.

As the aircraft, painted an unusual pink, rolled level with us in a billowing cloud of dust, I saw that its registration was *Foxtrot-Uniform-November*. On first impression, the occupants didn't look like much fun. The cabin door swung open and the pilot had climbed out, three inspectors following like a frown train. One of the team had already begun writing notes before even leaving the aircraft which seemed like a punch below the belt to me.

The team leader introduced himself as Mr Singh; he sported a spotless blue turban and a Barry White beard. His shoes were highly polished crocodile leather and his brown tie was definitely a '70s survivor. The footwear was both bad taste given our location in the reptile sanctuary of the Okavango and also just plain bad taste. I probably should have reported him to CITES and the fashion police.

At his side was a nervous looking young man carrying a clipboard, the same culprit who had been scribbling notes from inside the plane. I think this might have been his first experience of life in the field and he looked like the office would have been his preferred habitat. Mr Singh neglected to introduce his junior colleague.

Finally, like the odd man out in that game on the *Muppet Show,* was a Rastafarian who looked as though he had attended a hip business school. He was wearing a baggy suit straight from the Miami Vice wardrobe trailer with a T-shirt and flip flops on his bare feet.

'I'm Amos!' he called before collecting one of those measuring wheels that click off the metres as you walk. Those harmless looking contraptions have shut more airstrips and forced more alterations than any human

Shambolic

member of the air commission.

Mr Singh turned to me and said, 'So, let's have a look shall we?'

He sounded exactly like a doctor checking a rash that could have been avoided through better personal judgement. I glanced at Jackson to make sure he still had his trousers on, which he did, though his eyes were fixed with a covetous gaze on those crocodile shoes. I imagined there was some unlucky reptile out in the lagoon about to find itself skinned in the name of fashion brinkmanship.

As we started to pace, Mr Singh voiced his concerns about the proximity of the village which was on the boundary of the runway. As if to illustrate his concerns, a donkey ambled down the centre of the strip and a small child appeared to be digging a hole in the crumbly surface. I nodded in thoughtful agreement and the small team moved on.

'Jackson,' I summoned the airport manager in a suitably conspiratorial tone.

'Rra?' He was watching the shoes ahead of us.

'Maybe you can take this little one home?' I nodded towards the enthusiastic earthworm beside us.

Jackson wasn't considering the big picture, the need to impress our visitors, he was focussed on fashion. I nodded towards the village and my colleague reluctantly collected the child under his left arm in an unloving clasp. Chubby fingers reached back for the small hole into which I was kicking sandy turf as Jackson hauled him off towards the nearest group of huts.

'That isn't on the map!' called the young scribe ahead of us.

He pointed to a huge marula tree that stood like a sentry on one corner of the strip. He studied his map again and continued, 'This is the latest map and that tree isn't on it!'

Considering the great age of the tree, it had clearly been there long before the camp and the airstrip had been built, certainly longer than the junior bureaucrat had been alive. He should have been more concerned about the fact his predecessors had missed it on their own visits.

'That tree was growing there long before anyone thought to build this runway.'

I wanted to say something rational before we slipped deeper down the cartographic rabbit-hole. I turned to Singh as a more experienced inspector, I was pretty sure he would set the youngster straight.

'This is a ve-rrrrr serious issue!' was the reply, the rolling *R* emphasising just how serious.

'What's the problem? Just draw it onto your map now,' I suggested, though I knew as I said it that it was pointless, it was too sensible.

'We can't just alter a government map and that tree isn't supposed to be there!'

We were drifting into abstract theory, when is a tree not a tree? I glanced at Jackson, returned minus the infant, who had remained silent throughout and was ignoring our metaphysical chatter. His eyes continued to drift down to the crocodile shoes. I started to wonder if the tree that *wasn't a tree* might be the least of Mr Singh's worries; he might not get out of here with his footwear.

'The tree must be removed,' declared the chief inspector, '*at once!*'

He seriously thought it was simpler to remove an arboreal giant than to update a map with the flick of his pen.

'At once!' echoed the young scribe.

They were both clearly insane, lost in their inflexible maze of procedures and petty officialdom. I realised that the only way to fight nonsensical minion-think was with more of the same.

'I can't just cut that tree down,' I said, 'I need to inform the Wildlife Department and it is the property of the village, their committee needs to be consulted.'

This brought a dark frown to Mr Singh's face as he considered all the paperwork that would be generated by involving another government department in a discussion over an unauthorised tree and then the entire community chiming in. I was about to mention the tree had particular ceremonial significance, which was a lie, but Singh had come to a decision.

'Maybe we can just ignore it?' he ventured in a more conciliatory tone.

There was a child in a pair of ripped Adidas shorts watching from the edge of the village. He ran and looked up into the great Marula tree thinking we had seen something interesting in it. Why else would we all be standing around staring at a tree that apparently didn't exist? The tree remained stoically aloof, nature wisely ignores the petty confusions of mankind until on occasion it has to swat us back into line with an act of illuminating annihilation.

Amos the Rasta had already walked several hundred metres away from us, measuring with his little wheel. The tracks in the sand meandered from one side of the strip to the other; if this were the course of a river he would be in oxbow lake territory. At least I knew in advance that there would be an argument about the length of the runway which was meant to be exactly one kilometre. The tree was momentarily forgotten. We walked on and Mr Singh discussed things, in a stream of consciousness, with his staff. He pointed out problems, the scribe wrote them down and the Rasta rolled along in front of us. The child trailed behind us, wondering what we were doing on his playground. Jackson had disappeared off somewhere offering better shade.

Two hundred metres short of the threshold, the wheels literally fell off, or rather the wheel. Amos came to an abrupt stop and held up the measuring device which was now just a stick. He looked inquiringly at the end, momentarily at a loss.

'Oh dear!' said Mr Singh, 'the wheel's come off!'

His observational skills were as sharp as his shoes.

'Do you have a spare?' I asked because I wanted to get this wrapped up and get them gone.

'No,' said Singh patiently, 'each inspection team is allocated one wheel, they come from our supplier in Norway.'

Of course they did, where else would you buy a simple plastic measuring device if you lived in southern Africa?

'The screw broke and the wheel fell off!'

This comment came from the driver himself, delivered as final clarity on the situation.

There was momentary silence and I pictured a bunch of fur clad Vikings making these little devices in the frozen north. Not to be defeated, Amos fished around in his pocket for a moment and came out with a slim bolt and nut with which he fixed the wheel. I was most impressed and certainly Mr Singh had never seen such decisive work from a team member. This young man was destined for great things, promotion, senior government positions, the sky was the limit. The child continued along behind the hero of the hour whilst our small group idled mid-way along the airstrip.

Mr Singh spotted the airfield water pump, a machine we had installed after our last inspection and one, which I should mention, was a complete failure. The pump was there to water the strip daily during the long dry months of summer to help hold the surface together. At least that was the theory. The pump was meant to be attached to a pipe that stretched the entire length of the strip. Ours ran for about four metres before it had been dug up and the poly-pipe had been borrowed by some good citizen, probably to make the biggest bong in sub-Saharan Africa. If you did start the pump, a small pool of water would form about eighteen metres from the edge of the strip which the donkeys enjoyed, but which didn't quite meet with DCA regulations.

'Your irrigation system has an unusual design,' observed the team leader without a trace of sarcasm.

'Jackson designed it,' I said and the scribe duly wrote this down.

Glancing around I saw that our airport manager was relaxing in the shade of the marula tree, having his head groomed by one of the Donkey Deceptors. He really would have been a tremendous pharaoh in different times.

'How do you water the airstrip when the pipe ends here?'

This was a reasonable question.

'We use sprinklers and carry the pump along in a wheelbarrow,' I lied.

'Can we see the wheelbarrow?' Singh was playing hardball.

'It is being serviced at the moment,' I lied again and added, 'but we have ordered more pipes to improve the system.'

I made a mental note to do just that so that we really could water the strip, it seemed like the least I could do. If shame is life's reward for inactivity, then I should probably have felt that to some degree. Still, I only had to raise my eyes to gaze across the sun blazed landscape to be reminded of the undeniable distractions around me. The plumbing could wait, again.

Thankfully, before Singh could push the issue, the Rasta finished his measuring and returned with his findings on a piece of graph paper. He handed the paper to the office junior for perusal.

'Eh!' he said.

'Hmm!' added Singh who was looking over his shoulder.

'Your airstrip is of incorrect proportion,' he stated, 'we will have to assess whether it is viable to allow further air traffic to operate here.'

I suspect he imagined this was a terrible prospect for me but really, closing the airstrip meant no clients and staff drinking sessions at leisure.

'I see,' is what I actually said, 'what exactly is wrong?'

'Regulations state that an airstrip must be exactly one kilometre in length,' the chief explained. 'We find that your airstrip exceeds this distance by some 100 metres.'

'It's too long?'

These people were clearly on the lunatic fringe of officialdom.

'In short, yes, it is too long!' confirmed Mr Singh with a grave nod.

'So we need to shorten it?' I guessed.

'No!' replied crocodile shoes and both the scribe and I breathed a sigh of relief. 'You must alter your threshold markers so that it is obvious that the last 100 metres of the airstrip are, in fact, excess ground.'

It was beyond baffling and I had yet to meet a bush pilot with a complaint about having too much airstrip to aim for.

'My department will inform the air charter operators that they may no longer use that section of the...' Singh searched for the perfect words, 'old airfield.'

The time to argue was long gone and I shepherded them back towards their own aircraft. Jackson noticed our direction of travel and rejoined us for a final longing gaze at those fancy loafers.

Before they left, I was asked to move a goat kraal that had been built too close to the strip. As we passed it Mr Singh waved at the old man working there who waved back nervously. After all, everyone knows the DCA are crazy. The soon-to-be-promoted Amos packed his wheel into the luggage pod and the inspection team climbed back into their aircraft in reverse seniority. The scribe was squeezed right into the back of the cabin. His eyes were tightly shut as the Cessna started up the strip. I didn't blame him. He had, after all, spent much of his day discovering the many flaws in our remote aerodrome. It was a very warm day and the aircraft slowly clawed its way free of the earth, wheels skimming the papyrus as it banked across the lagoon. Jackson spat at the ground, the engine drone receded to nothing and we walked to the shade of the old marula tree to share a cigarette.

It might not have been real, that tree, but we all liked it just the same.

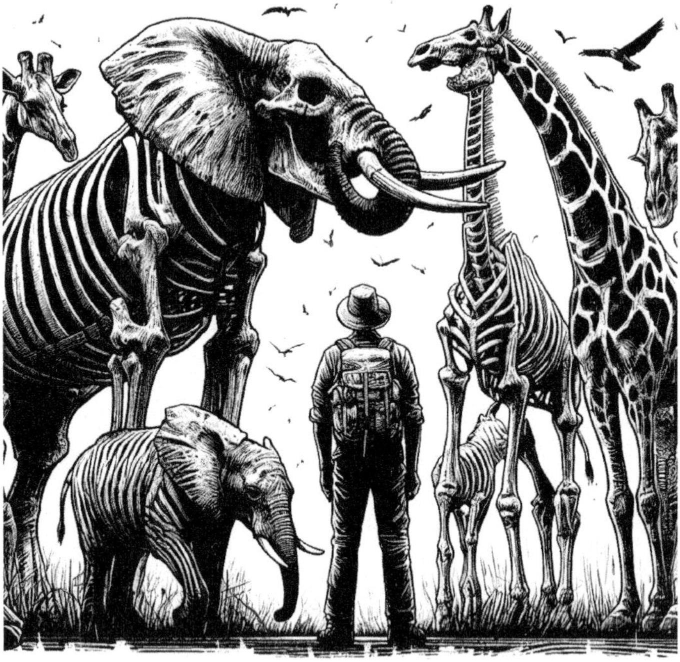

The Guide's Guide
to Guides' Exams

You might think the Botswana government had better ways to spend taxpayers money than checking on the precise measurements of remote airfields. As a matter of fact, they did not. We frequently had officials from various state departments drifting into camp asking for relevant documentation. It was a good way to access the bar and chat up the staff for a start. It could be tricky though if you happened to lack a crucial piece of official paperwork, like a guide's licence for example.

In the step up from construction crew to camp guide, I hadn't had the opportunity to sit the national guides' exam. One of my friends had already been busted in the Moremi Game Reserve whilst driving a Land Rover full of camera-toting tourists.

'These people in the back of my Land Rover officer? Just some family and close friends out for some fresh air…' Just a matter of time before the dragnet closed in.

It was a relief when confirmation chirped down the radio that Okavango Wilderness Safaris was sponsoring my guide's licence exam in Maun. Having already been employed as a guide for some three months, it was time to make it official. The national exam only runs a couple of times a year, so you miss it and you have to wait. Bleak rumour had it that our exam was being set and invigilated by Zimbabwean guide instructors, which was bad news as they knew their stuff. They also had a reputation to protect and wouldn't be passing weak candidates.

First of all though, I had to get to Maun from Jedibe which was hidden away in the heart of the Okavango Delta. There was no flight available for a lowly illegal guide so I took a speedboat an hour up the river to a spot known as the Duba Boat Station. This was a grand name for a patch of sand which was just large enough to haul the bow of a boat onto. The next section of the journey involved paddling a mokoro across a wide, muddy lagoon, criss-crossed with hippo trails and clogged with papyrus. That took about twenty wobbly minutes. A friend was waiting on the other side with a Land Rover which we were driving to Maun. As we had to collect a few other staff members en route, the drive took us about seven hours in total. Seven hours of grinding through thick sand and surging across flooded channels. We were all sunburned and dehydrated by the time we reached town, ready for a bad night of sleep at the mosquito ridden company plot before our big day.

To further improve our chances of success, we went straight to the nearest bar and drank until midnight as it was such a novelty to be out of the bush for a few days. We were a sorry looking bunch when Chris, the ops director, gave us a pre-exam briefing in the first light of morning. It was meant to be one of those morale-boosting presentations, the reputation of the company rested with us and what a wonderful opportunity we all had. In the end, he just shook his head and told us not to miss the start of the first session before heading back to his office muttering dark phrases.

The guides' exams are held at the Wildlife Sanctuary in Maun, a scrubby little nature reserve with a few government buildings scattered about. The format of the day included various written exams, a formal interview and finally a guided walk where you had to try to impress your examiner with the great depth of your knowledge. The written papers were pretty straightforward. We then listened to recordings of bird and animal calls to try and ID them. That was followed by a session in the infamous bone room; tables covered in animal parts, skins, scales, teeth and so on. You would pick up a bone fragment and try to think of a vaguely sensible identification. It's easy when you are dealing with elephants and hippos but medium sized antelope all start to look the same. Everything on the planet, when deconstructed into component parts, morphs from the obvious collective to the obscure individual. Everyone knows what a zebra looks like, very few people know what they look like under the stripes, the meat and the muscle.

We gathered for a short huddle after the lunch break and before the all-important bush walk. It is never good for your mental state to discuss your answers before the end of the day.

'Did you guys spot that genet incisor on table three?'

'Genet? Genet! I thought that was a sodding crocodile tooth!'

'At least those acacia bark samples were easy.'

'I didn't see any acacia samples, it was all albidias and mopane...'

Having increased our stress levels with a little competitive self-assessment, we sat, shared cigarettes and waited to be called by a walk examiner. There were certain invigilators that, rumour had it, were tougher than others. One particular man had a perma-frown and carried himself with the loping stride of an alpha predator. He was practically staring the candidates down as he walked amongst them, daring someone to try and communicate with him.

'Not him,' I said to myself, 'anyone but him...'

In contrast, there was a friendly looking woman with a shoulder patch identifying her as a senior guide trainer from Botswana.

'Her, let it be her!'

The couple stood side by side and looked at us, the frown and the smile.

'Forbes!' barked the frown.

'Oh for fuck's sake!' I muttered and the sentiment was echoed by a couple of my mates.

The examiner and I walked into the reserve where the following hour passed in a blur. I rambled on about the plants and trees we saw, medicinal uses, Latin names, protected status under local law, construction uses, you name it, I threw it into the mix. The main problem with the reserve in Maun is that the very few wild animals unfortunate enough to live there had long fled from the racket of the examination process. I was probably candidate eighty to walk that trail and there wasn't a living thing to be seen which made it hard to deliver an exciting interpretative

Shambolic

bush walk. After twenty minutes I was wishing I had held back some of my amazing flora knowledge.

'Pace!' warned Mr Happy, as we arrived at a small clearing containing an area of long grass. The grass had been partially flattened.

'Thoughts?' asked the frown, as he indicated the flat spot.

I sensed a trap. Obviously, it was meant to be the resting spot of some animal. We had seen nothing and there were no tracks to study aside from boot prints of the various humans wandering about. What does live in this dump anyway, I thought to myself, a donkey? A vagrant? Why hadn't we thought to come here last week to check the place out and learn something useful about the reserve? I was stumped and then I saw the corner of a plywood board poking out from the bushes next to us. Really? Could it be that simple? I decided to gamble that he had a sense of humour.

'I think this was the resting place for that piece of wood,' pointing to the board on the ground, fully committed.

A very small smile touched the edges of the frown and he turned to continue walking down the trail. Later, I heard at least one other candidate mention the wooden board and I sensed it was going to be okay. I was right.

Two weeks later I was able to legitimately guide my clients in Botswana, just like I had been doing for months.

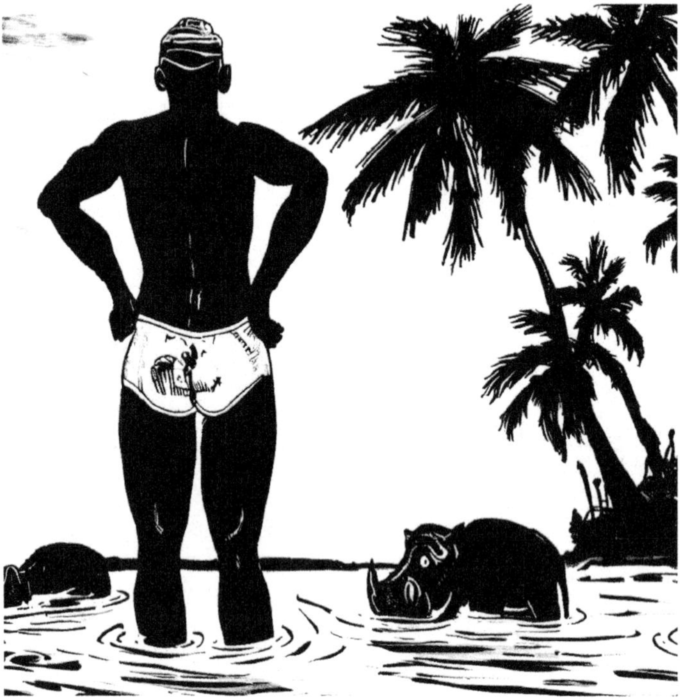

The Trouble with George

'Eh base, base, base for George.' The radio handset crackled in the small office at Jedibe Island Camp.

'Base here, go ahead George.'

'Ah, I got a big *matata* here, please come and see!' said George.

'What is the problem George?'

'Aish! Come and see this *matata* please,' continued George cryptically, 'I got a big problem here!'

'Can I have some details, George?'

'Oh! I got a problem with my outboard, a big problem…' George gave me a hint.

Looking at the guides' schedule for the day, I saw that George was on his way back from dropping guests at the airstrip on a neighbouring island. That at least told me roughly where he was even if George himself was keeping a lid on the finer details of his major *matata*.

'OK, George, sit tight. I'm on my way.'

There was no reply so I dropped the handset back on the radio base unit, picked up a handheld radio from the desk charger and walked down to the boat station. On my way through the kitchen I saw Aukie, one of the camp managers, and explained where I was going.

'What's up with George?' she asked and I shrugged with open palms because I indeed had no idea what the problem was with George.

In a water camp like Jedibe, guides have relatively few pieces of equipment for which they are responsible. There are no expensive Land Rovers to shed costly parts across the countryside. No complex vehicle radio systems to expose to rain in a puff of fuse-blowing calamity. No powerful spotlights to drop and reverse over on night drives. A guide at Jedibe Island Camp just needs a handheld radio, an aluminium boat that floats and an outboard engine to propel the whole package along the beautiful waterways of the Okavango Delta. George had already confirmed his radio worked and his boat was apparently still floating so I collected a tool kit from the workshop in preparation for what I assumed was a hammer and wrench rescue.

The camp's small fleet was tied up in the shade of a huge marula tree. Their frequently dinged bows rested on a shallow bank which doubled as our cleaning and maintenance station. I reversed my own boat out of the line in a faint mist of outboard fumes, the official territorial display of all heavily used petrol engines. Then I turned the longbow into clean air before gliding across the mirror calm lagoon, nosing between hundreds of water lilies towards the narrow entrance hidden in a wall of thick papyrus. This secret portal opened onto the deep-water channel beyond. Turn left for the airstrip and George's problem or right for the mighty Okavango and adventure beyond your wildest imaginings. I'd be lying if I didn't give the latter some thought, but I went left and poured on the throttle to start looking for my colleague who was apparently drifting helpless as a freshly hatched crocodile on the river currents.

It only took five minutes to find him, standing in his boat midstream with slumped shoulders and a look of great consternation on his usually cheerful face. I couldn't help but notice that of the two main pieces of equipment for which George was the principal supervisor, one was clearly absent. The transom shone dully in the bright sunshine, enjoying the exposure it was generally denied by the large outboard engine we bolted to it. Which wasn't there. The only thing inside the boat was George.

'George,' I began, 'where is your outboard?'

It seemed like a totally reasonable question under the circumstances. He turned his gaze back to the uncluttered transom as if searching for something, like an outboard engine perhaps, before clearing his throat thoughtfully.

'Aah! Well… I was driving back from the airstrip,' I was getting the long version of events, 'and when I came around this corner,' he pointed for the sake of clarity, 'I noticed that the engine wasn't bolted onto my boat anymore.'

Curious indeed, could an otter with a monkey wrench have been up to no good?

There was more though and George continued, 'There was a strange noise and then the engine went over my head and into the river!'

George swivelled his gaze bleakly to the silty waters swirling beside us.

'What happened to the mounting bolts?'

Every outboard was held in place by four heavy-duty bolts to prevent exactly this kind of situation. There was no sign of sheared bolts, just four neat empty holes where they used to be.

'Ah, *those* bolts!' replied George enthusiastically as he poked a finger through one of the holes as if searching for clues. After a couple of silent seconds, George realised that I wasn't done with that line of questioning and admitted, 'Well, I think I might have used them to put a new door in my sister's house.'

'So what was holding the outboard down?' he must have anticipated that one.

'I used this very strong rope,' he showed me the remains of a frayed nylon cord, the sort favoured by tramps as dog leads or trouser belts.

'This is strong rope, number one, no problem here!' George was working hard to win me over in the rope versus bolt debate.

'Sure,' I replied, 'there is nothing wrong with that rope.' His face lit up like a lottery winner, 'except that it isn't four bolts, it broke and your engine fell in the river!'

No reply.

'How do you think we can get the engine back?'

I pondered the question George least wanted to hear. He would probably have given me money for a new outboard rather than submerge himself in the murky crocodile rich water.

'Maybe some boys from the village can look for it?' ventured George.

Shambolic

If I had suggested we tie a rope around his grandmother and drop her over the side he probably would have gone to collect her personally.

'Sorry, George, but you are going over the side as soon as we locate the thing.'

I spun my boat and roared back to camp to get some help whilst he considered his options. I knew he would be waiting when I returned as he had no way of escaping, not with his outboard resting on the bottom of the river. I have no idea exactly what George did whilst I gathered a small team of searchers and boats from the camp, but I suspect prayer may have been involved.

To his credit, not only was George still in his powerless vessel when we returned but he had stripped to his underpants, clearly accepting his duty as our rescue diver. It is fair to say that had his lower lip dropped any further he could have tripped over it and straight into the water.

We spread out across the channel in four boats and started probing the riverbed with ngashis, the long poles used to punt mekoros. I was hoping we would make contact with something other than catfish and crocodiles in the area George had last seen his precious outboard. After half an hour of stirring up silt, it was beginning to look hopeless and George was in much better spirits. Then a boat that had drifted some three hundred metres downstream made contact with the hard plastic shell, raising a shout from the crew. Either the engine had continued to motor along underwater or George wasn't quite as observant a guide as he should have been.

It was time for action and the mood shifted up a gear as George was handed a long rope to tie around the outboard's prop arm. His friends gave him hearty slaps on the back and cheery encouragement. At times like this, the humans who get to stay in the boat are quite happy to let their less fortunate comrade know that they are really glad to be staying topside.

'Good luck, George!'
'Try not to drown, George!'
'Try not to get eaten by a crocodile, George!'
'Can I have your shoes if you don't come back?'

Taking a deep breath, clasping the rope with eyes tightly shut, Botswana's own Cousteau threw himself off the side of the boat. The deepest parts of that river are about six metres deep, but George managed to hit a sandbank. Picture a man, body tensed like a spring, eyes screwed shut crouching in knee deep water, in his underpants. Not so much Tarzan in the jungle as delicate Jane in the bath. Some of the guys nearly fell out of their boats, they were laughing so hard. Our intrepid underwater explorer opened his eyes and scowled, robbed of all glory but still in mortal danger. Rather than stay and listen to the derision, he plunged into deeper water and swam to the pole marking the outboard's resting place. One final defiant look at the peanut gallery before he ducked under the swirling surface.

Incredibly, George managed to get the loop of rope around the prop on his first attempt. That done, he practically walked back across the water and into the nearest boat.

'Well done, George!'

I felt that someone should acknowledge his achievement even if some of the crew looked a bit disappointed that nothing had actually happened to him. George pulled his clothes back on as our little convoy headed back to camp and the outboard lay on the floor of my boat, leaking water like the drowned thing that it was.

Once we were all safely back at base, the rescue team disappeared except for George who was anxious to see the extent of the damage. We surveyed the engine together, now propped up outside our small workshop. It was coated in river weed and sand, it looked broken. Sakkie, our staff manager came to join us, attracted by the drama which for once had nothing to do with him.

We didn't have a manual for George's 55 hp Mariner but, after rifling the workshop, we found one for a Yamaha outboard. I reasoned that they were the same shape, did the same job on the same fuel, so repairing them should follow similar procedures. In the troubleshooting section there was a heading, 'In case of total freshwater submersion', perfect. It explained, 'Should your outboard be totally immersed for a period in excess of two minutes, the engine may seize unless all water residue and foreign objects are cleaned from working parts. This must be completed before a period of two hours since immersion has elapsed.' It failed to mention the best way to go about achieving this; that way the engine would seize and you would have to buy another one from them. I looked up at George's worried face and Sakkie's apparent joy at being involved. We were about to make amateur outboard repair history, right there under the warm Okavango sun.

Removing the spark plugs and inverting the outboard allowed half a litre of river water to pour from the empty sockets. Cranking the engine gear led to the carburettor coughing up a small sandcastle. It reminded me of an unlucky bodysurfer I had once seen in France, throwing up a sizable portion of the Atlantic after a serious thrashing by Poseidon. Those were the obvious boxes ticked, but I knew that somewhere inside the drowned engine there had to be more water. A vague memory from some school science class resurfaced, something to do with the hygroscopic properties of ethanol. I didn't have a bottle of ethanol handy but I did have access to plenty of its extended family tree. Sakkie was dispatched to fetch a bottle of vodka. If it could do to our engine what it had done to millions of Russian livers, then we might be okay.

After a couple of minutes, he returned to say the bar was out of vodka.

'Bring any clear alcohol,' I explained, 'gin, cane, anything will do!'

Sakkie and George exchanged a pitying glance, they assumed I was sun-touched.

'A can of beer?' ventured Sakkie.

'No, bring the gin, please!'

They looked at each other again and Sakkie shrugged before heading back to the bar. He came back with a broad smile and a double gin on ice.

'Sakkie, I don't want to drink it!' I pointed to the outboard, 'it's for the engine!'

'Ah! For the engine!'

Sakkie repeated with a look of complete incomprehension on his face before heading back for the rest of the bottle. I drank the well chilled booze to pass the time until he returned with the mother lode.

With a pang of guilt, I poured two thirds of a bottle of Gordon's down the carburettor and cranked it back out of the spark plug sockets. Gin is the backbone of expatriate societies across the globe and abusing it like this really was a shame. At this point, Sakkie and George were just humouring me, expecting me to stick a slice of lemon in the outlet pipe. The last ingredient to my mecha-voodoo cocktail was a slug of light oil for the patient. As it trickled out of sight to coat gears and other useful parts, I considered the wording of the report I would have to write for HQ, requesting a new outboard. George saw an opportunity to assist and went to find some replacement bolts for those he had gifted to his sister's house.

We lifted the dead weight engine back into place, screwed the bolts on tight and gave the fuel injection system a clean petrol flush. That was the extent of my abilities, every card played and the firewater gamble was still likely to come up snake eyes. Sakkie screwed the spark plugs back into place, George screwed his eyes shut again and I gave the starter rope a good pull. To our collective amazement, the engine started. As the rich mixture of petrol, oil and gin fogged the air with an alcoholic blue haze, George started dancing for joy. He had probably imagined his paycheck being docked for the next decade whilst he paid off the damage. Sakkie picked up the bottle of mother's ruin, regarded the contents with awe and declared, 'Gordon's number one bush mechanic!' I expect this might have started a craze in the village with people pouring England's finest into everything from rusty generators to difficult babies. There isn't much that a bottle of gin can't sort out when the chips are down.

Less than a month later, Sakkie would dwarf George's minor *matata* and an ocean of hooch wouldn't rectify the disaster.

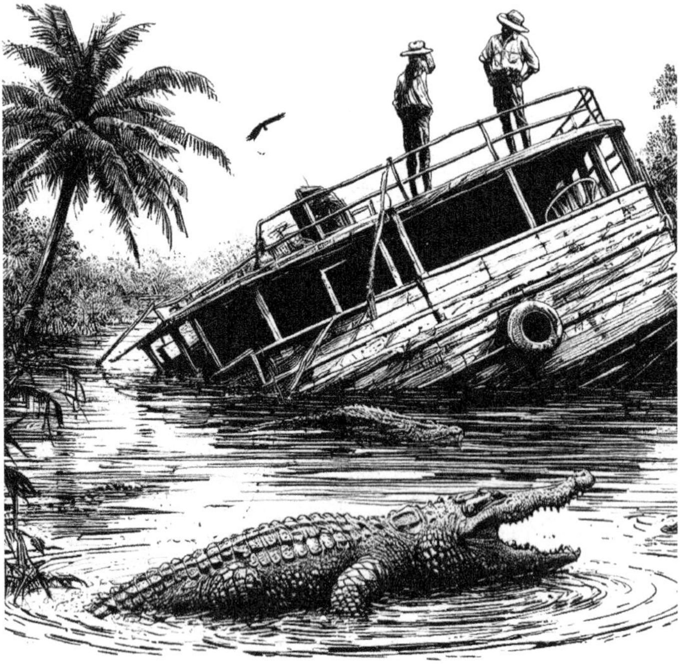

The Wreck of the Black Crake

Jedibe Island Camp, as the name suggests, lacked any road connections. The only way to deliver freight was on a barge. There was a barge and a barge driver specifically for this purpose. It was a major event when his wide-hulled vessel chugged into our lagoon every couple of months. The skipper sat on a raised platform in the stern, under one of those umbrellas you get in outdoor bars in city centres. A bit like Bogart in the *African Queen* except he delivered our booze, he didn't just drink it. He also brought us kitchen supplies, workshop equipment and news from the outside world. It was a good system most of the time, until one month when the barge was double booked.

A hunting party up in the pan handle got our usual slot on the schedule. This was a problem as we needed a major resupply for a camp full of hungry guests. Our replenishment from Maun was scheduled to arrive upstream, where it would slowly perish in the hot sun or just be liberated by anyone fortunate enough to live near the small dock.

Gypsy and I met in the bar which was where we did our best thinking. The solution presented itself in the unlikely but amiable form of our staff manager, Sakkie, who in his own words was a genuine 'BaYei water bushman'. We decided that he would take the camp's double decker boat, The Black Crake, on this unique occasion to collect our supplies.

The Black Crake was typically only used for booze cruises close to camp but a barge or a houseboat? Is there a difference?

'He'll be fine,' Gypsy commented as our trusted captain headed back to the staff village, 'he's got magic.' Like many facts he shared, it was unexpected but stated with absolute confidence.

'Magic?'

'Sure. Sakkie is the village sangoma.'

Fair enough, why wouldn't he be? I'd been working with Sakkie for almost a year and never once had I suspected he had a supernatural side hustle.

'He just has to follow the river and collect the freight.'

It seemed like a task he was fit for, regardless.

'Hmm.' Gypsy mused aloud, 'Dancing is his thing anyway.'

Our planning session had drifted well off piste but it wasn't boring.

'Like trance dancing?'

'Exactly, he has a reed skirt, spins around for hours and blows cigarette smoke all over the patient. He's good.'

Gypsy delivered that last opinion as he climbed off his bar stool and walked off in the same direction as the shaman. Was he a good witch doctor or just a good dancer? It didn't matter, he just had to follow the river and come home with the loot.

As the first rays of sunlight played across the morning Okavango mist, Sakkie and his two-man crew loaded one hundred litres of petrol and a cooler box full of sandwiches onto the houseboat to begin their voyage. The load they needed to collect was sizable; 800 litres of petrol, 100 litres of outboard oil, four solar panels, twenty cases of red wine, twenty cases of white wine, freezer boxes of fresh meat and a mountain of dry food. The Black Crake had two large deck spaces but we had warned Sakkie not to load anything onto the upper deck as this wouldn't help stability on a vessel already prone to leaning a little on sharp bends. The houseboat had twin forty hp outboards which propelled it at a fairly leisurely pace.

As we watched the dawn patrol edging out of the glass smooth lagoon, everything looked pretty good. We just had to wait for Sakkie to radio us at the end of his twelve-hour cruise. All that done, we went and did some fishing before the working day began.

The following morning, Sakkie radioed as planned. He had reached the loading station despite using more fuel than expected and he would have to use some of the camp's supply on the return journey. What he really meant was, as soon as he was out of sight he had loaded thirty villagers onto the houseboat and charged them for the ride up the river. The boat being so heavily laden with domestic tourists, he ran out of fuel. If there was any petrol left over he probably would have flogged that along the riverbank. Our very own Magellan also told us that the supply truck hadn't arrived yet, shorthand for, 'I'm going to party in the village!' Sakkie was something of a dude and was no doubt telling a wide-eyed village virgin that the boat was his and if she played her cards right, he'd take her for a cruise sometime. None of this was a surprise, we still had faith in our chosen captain and *guesstimated* that he would arrive back at Jedibe late the following day.

As the sun began to dip below the tallest palms the following day, we didn't hear the welcome sound of the Black Crake motoring towards camp; we heard nothing but reed frogs and mosquitoes. After several attempts to raise Sakkie on the radio, his voice eventually crackled back across the ether. A few probing questions helped us build a better picture of the state of play. He wasn't en route, he was still at the loading dock and furthermore, in his own words, 'The Crake isn't floating very nicely'. Sakkie suggested that we might need a new plan, due to the slight *matata* he had encountered.

This was disappointing news because Sakkie and The Black Crake *were* our new plan, a fact I pointed out to him only to be rewarded with a lengthy silence. It could be tricky getting a straight answer from Sakkie face-to-face; over a crackling radio link, there was zero possibility of matata resolution. Gypsy and I looked at each other, hopes fading as fast as the light.

'OK, Sakkie, sit tight. I'm coming to you.'

Even if our reserve-barge was going to limp home, we were pretty sure we could handle the freight with the various boats in camp, but it would require more manpower than we could spare from the guiding team. I would have to get upstream to assess and make a plan from there so it

Shambolic

was early to bed in preparation for a very long day.

It isn't wise being on the water before sunrise because of hippo activity. Nevertheless, I puttered gently into Jedibe village in the dark. There was a local fisherman I planned to take along as the loading station was many hours beyond my navigational knowledge and I didn't have time to get lost. As my bow touched the pale sandy shoreline, a figure detached from the darkness to step aboard, hand raised in silent greeting he huddled into a blanket and went straight to sleep on the deck. Excellent, though I wouldn't need his help for at least six hours so I shoved in my earpods and turned up the motivational chanting of *The Offspring*. By early afternoon, after hours of motoring full throttle past endless papyrus lined side channels and skimming around sandbanks, we were no closer to finding signs of the houseboat.

'Are we definitely in the right channel?' I asked as once again the waterway split into several options.

'Eh, just keep right on here,' replied the perma-dozing tracker, waving his hand casually in a wide radius that could have meant any one of them.

Half an hour later, we were low on fuel and had long run out of anything cold to drink. That was when we rounded a wide river bend and found a festival in full swing. I dropped the throttle and let the boat settle back into the current, marvelling at the thoroughly surreal scene spread out before me. The riverbank was a hive of activity with groups of people dancing or sitting around cooking fires. The warm air was filled with the sound of kwaito blasting from a hi-fi attached to a car battery.

I swung the boat closer to the bank and called out to see if anyone had seen the houseboat. An old man wearing a dirty raincoat and not much else staggered down to the water's edge. He gave a joyful wave, swept his arm upriver like a traffic policeman and lifted a bottle of red wine to his smiling lips. Now that I was closer to the action, I started to notice a little more detail in this picnic pastiche. There were bags of rice being cooked with tabasco sauce, Jacob's crackers being dipped into jars of marmalade and a child had his entire fist buried in a jar of Marmite. These things didn't typically feature in the average diet of Botswana's rural villagers; clearly the looting had begun in earnest. My guide was wide awake now and stood in amazement, chuckling out loud as if he had woken in the middle of an especially good dream. Nero would have approved.

Three more bends in the river and we found the houseboat. Sakkie's original complaint that The Black Crake wasn't floating nicely was something of an understatement. The boat had lost all tendency towards buoyancy some time ago. Sakkie himself was there to meet us, waving from his perch on the bottom of the hull which was now the roof, the actual roof being somewhere beneath five feet of river water.

'Do you see my problem?' shouted Sakkie in greeting, worried that I hadn't grasped the severity of the situation.

'It looks like the houseboat is upside down?'

'Yes!' he seemed relieved that I had been able to identify his predicament, 'that is my problem!'

My mute river guide gave a low whistle and shook his head, 'Aish! Matata!'

'You aren't fucking kidding…' I added pointlessly.

We tied up to the railings of the lower deck which were just poking clear of the water and climbed up the side of the hulk to join Sakkie. Disappointingly, the situation didn't look any better from up there. Still, it is a unique sensation to be sitting on an inverted houseboat in the middle of the Okavango River.

'What happened, Sakkie?'

Our horse had definitely bolted but I would have to shape some sort of report in the near future.

'Well, the truck came yesterday and we started to put the freight downstairs, the fuel drums, the food, everything on the bottom deck, just like our plan.'

Sakkie had clearly decided to illustrate that he was sticking to the rules set out in the camp bar. He was also remarkably relaxed, suggesting that he may have found a bottle of liberated wine himself. That, or he'd just been dancing in the firelight, purging his own demons.

'Then what happened?' I prompted because he had glazed over a bit and was gazing into the middle distance, at nothing in particular.

'Ah!' he was back with me for a moment, 'then we wave bye-bye to the truck driver and go this way out into the river.'

He steered his hand through the air like an imaginary boat to show me the reverse direction of travel.

Then, in a serious tone of voice with a grave expression, he continued,

'Someone say that the floor is very wet downstairs and they are too worried about the kwena,' his head shook at the thought of it, like a trauma victim in regression therapy. 'I say that the crocodile is only in the river, but that man shout that he is worried that we *are* going into the river!'

'Why was the floor wet, Sakkie?'

Fascinating as his tale was, it was quite vague. His eyes swivelled towards me with a puzzled look, as if this was a pointless line of questioning.

'I don't know because I can't see from the top deck, so I try to drive back to the boat station.'

This news was delivered with a fierce frown to show just how hard he had tried, 'but the boat make like this!'

Sakkie used his hand again to depict a diving motion.

'When we are near the bank, the boat started to go on the side and everyone jumped off!'

'Couldn't you have reversed into the dock?'

I delivered this question more to the universe than any particular human in it, it didn't really matter either way.

'Oh no! I jumped off as well because of the kwena!'

The skipper looked at me like I was nuts for suggesting he try and save the situation.

'Then *The Crake* fell over and I radioed you!'

'Aish!' commented the tracker in wide-eyed astonishment at the epic proportions of the catastrophe.

'Aish in fucking-deed!' I muttered down to the river god.

In translation, all of the freight had been chucked onto the front of the lower deck, the part closest to the dock, quick and easy. When The Black Crake was reversed out into the insistent current, the water started to flow over the flat bow and along the lower deck. This resulted in some conversation about crocodiles and no one tried to redistribute the load along the deck. That might have tipped the balance back in

Sakkie's favour. As soon as the nervous skipper powered forwards into the current, he became Botswana's very first submariner. Not only that, but what freight hadn't fallen into the water had apparently been heisted by the locals. Shipwrecks have always been a gift to remote communities but usually the captain makes some attempt to rescue the cargo, not just drink it.

'Did you manage to save anything?' I wasn't sure I wanted the answer.

'Sure! Plenty!' Sakkie pointed enthusiastically to the bank where the crew had piled two dozen soaked boxes which they were now sleeping next to.

The most depressing thing was that the boat had sunk so close to the bank that it was possible to step across without getting wet. I poked through the remaining supplies which consisted of burst bags of rice and pasta, cans of soft drinks which were already getting rusty from the heat and a five-litre bottle of cooking oil. The only thing left for us was to check the hull for anything that hadn't been washed away. It was pretty obvious that the local hunter-gatherers weren't going to leave anything for us on our next visit.

'OK chaps!' I stood and started to unbutton my shirt, 'we are going into the water to look for freight.'

The dozing crew sat up in shock and Sakkie suddenly found his focus. A kamikaze pilot stopping for hitch hikers couldn't have induced a stronger reaction.

'Too much kwena in there!' was the unanimous reply and the crew hunkered down to shake heads and mutter mutinously amongst themselves. I expect that captains often face this sort of negative groupthink after a shipwreck, what they needed was some motivation.

'You can get in the water with me,' I explained, 'or you can walk home!'

Jedibe was a few days' hard struggle through big game swamp. The ultimatum resulted in a miserably slow partial disrobing on behalf of the crew. Sakkie, grinning like the lunatic holy man he was, stripped naked. The contraband liquor was getting to his head in the hot sun.

'Why don't you leave your shorts on in case some ladies walk by?' I suggested to my stoned and naked staff manager. Sakkie looked like he wished some ladies *would* walk by but, reluctantly, put his shorts back on.

Shambolic

That done, we climbed back onto the houseboat and looked for the safest place to enter the water. Given that the Okavango Delta can produce crocodiles of anything up to five metres in length, that was a forlorn hope. I lowered myself tentatively into the boat, hanging from the upper deck railings with my feet on a solar panel. My fearless aquanauts clearly weren't going to move until I was submerged, so they could gauge the potential risk to themselves. If I was dragged straight to hell by a scaly leviathan, they would head back to the party in the village. If not, their pride would eventually force them to join me.

Fully committed, I dropped off the railing and found myself at eye level with the murky river. I waited, motionless, to see if I would be killed outright. After ten long seconds I still wasn't dead, so the crew reluctantly climbed into the upturned hull with me. When this still failed to provoke fury from Sobek's local representatives, we began probing the bottom of the boat which was actually the ceiling of the lower deck.

Everyone was extremely skittish. As contact was made with a piece of furniture or a six pack of beer, the owner of the probing foot would howl and jump. They would then have to go back to try and relocate the inanimate object that had scared the shit out of them. This went on for a painful twenty minutes as the pile of salvage grew considerably on the bank. Because the river flowed into the open bow of the hull and out the stern, whenever something buoyant was kicked loose, it would pop up and drift away with the current. In this fashion we donated to the local community no less than five seat cushions, a life jacket, a bright blue cooler box and something that looked like one of those dachshund balloons that children's entertainers make.

Slowly, we cleared our way through the boat, initially somewhat protected by the side railings. Then continually edging closer to the unprotected bow which was just a broad gap into which the channel poured. The crew were lagging behind. I was feeling blasé, having been in the turbulent water for half an hour and not being killed once. Then I noticed what I hoped was driftwood but knew was a crocodile drifting down the channel side of the hull. It was a leisurely piece of inspection, more of a recce than an ambush. From eye level though, crocodilian reconnaissance and attack are very hard to distinguish. Thinking about that subtle dividing line is something better done from dry land. Even our earliest ancestors understood that logic.

I realised my reactions were glacially slow when I hauled myself clear of the water and saw the rest of the crew three metres up the bank in full scale retreat. From our vantage point we watched as the alpha predator in the neighbourhood turned and swam back up the side of the hull, his prehistoric snout carving a v-shaped bow wave before submerging next to the bow. That was the end of our salvage operation and the last time I was getting wet for a six-pack of warm beer. My final act was to cut free the one outboard still above river level. If anyone wanted what was left, they were welcome to it but they would have to get wet.

As we motored slowly past the carnival downstream, it was evident that the free bar had taken effect. Dancing was minimal and the level of unconsciousness was maximum. On the bank, the old man in the raincoat spotted us and ran along the water's edge until we were out of sight. He was waving the lifejacket in the air and shouting, 'Thank you! Thank you!'

That wasn't the end for our ill-fated booze cruiser. A month later, the head office decided that The Black Crake should be raised from the deep and recommissioned into our miniscule fleet. Cynically, I suspected that was a neat way to score on the insurance and reclaim the asset. To this end, a heavy barge and a truck-crane were deployed. The duo rolled the wreck and lifted it to the surface as easily as Sakkie had originally sunk it. It wasn't a pretty sight with a hull full of silt, the paint bubbling and the rails rusting. The barge then towed the hulk upstream to Seronga village for a refit at the hands of the only man who wanted the task.

Dop lived on the banks of the Okavango in his canvas workshop; a large army tent with crates of tools piled in the corners and a collection of bedding gathered around the central roof support. It was damp, gloomy and slightly depressing. The entire operation looked mobile and I couldn't work out if Dop was permanently resident or a nomadic tradesman. I assumed that, as he could technically live anywhere, he lived where he did because he liked it. Either way, he was now employed to raise our sorry vessel from the dead.

'I'll build you a different kind of boat!' He explained whilst we sat on the riverbank to survey the wreck. I didn't ask what that meant exactly but looking around at the chaotic camp he shared with his family, my expectations weren't especially high. Dop's clan consisted of a wife, a teenage son and daughter. The boy was clearly his understudy, fetching pieces of kit and listening to our discussions on the project. He was introduced as Jaco. When I glanced at the women, they ducked back behind the tent and Dop didn't bother to continue the introductions. This was his private domain so I focussed on the maintenance list for the boat and agreed to return in a fortnight to check his progress. It was almost full dark by the time I motored back into Jedibe's lagoon and the lantern lit camp looked like Manhattan compared to Dop's unloved home.

Various spares were despatched by truck from Maun to Seronga in the following days; paint stripper, paint, a new steering linkage and two brand new forty hp outboard engines. On the agreed day, I blasted back upstream with a couple of brief diversions to cast a fly across various junctions in the channel. Tiger fishing season was in full swing and it was a pleasure to have a legitimate reason to hunt a few down in the Delta's panhandle. It was past midday when I reached Dop's camp and, whilst The Black Crake was still hauled up the bank, there was no sign of the man himself. I climbed into the houseboat and saw that it had been scrubbed clean, most of the damaged paint was gone but the mechanical spares were still boxed and stacked on the lower deck. Truthfully, we weren't really missing the old tub in camp, we had enough boats to entertain the punters.

'Goeie more meneer!' Dop announced his arrival. He was dressed in blue overalls, barefoot and carrying a bottle of Castle Lager.

'Howzit Dop. Quiet around here today?' I indicated his silent camp and he shrugged.

'The wife's seeing Jaco off.'

'Where's he off to?' I hoped he was heading to school somewhere.

'The boy's sixteen now, the bus is dropping him at the border,' explained Dop, 'he can make his own way now.'

'When is he coming back?'

Dop shrugged again and disappeared into the gloom of the tent. Tough love or maybe just tough luck?

We spent the afternoon removing the rusted old steering linkage and cleaning the throttle cables. The limited conversation didn't stray beyond technical matters and the benefits of Japanese outboards over the cheaper Chinese versions. At sunset, Dop's daughter appeared with bowls of mieliepap in fish sauce, before wordlessly heading back to the tent. I was curious how she filled her days on the edge of the swamps but asking her father was evidently pointless. Seronga was a small village which I knew had a primary school and a National Parks and Wildlife office amongst other government facilities. Slim pickings for a social life but better than nothing.

It was too dark to work and Dop was clearly finished for the day as he stood, collected the empty bowls and said, 'Goeie nag.' If there was a guest suite, I guess it was occupied so I made a bed out of the long bench cushions. I'd known I would be stuck there for the night so I had packed a mosquito net in my rucksack. The transparent gauze separated me from the clouds of ravenous insects that haunted the riverbank. On consideration, I preferred my temporary quarters to the airless tent. The reality was that, in Dop's world, the most valuable object in the vicinity was the shitty old houseboat I was sleeping in. It also looked to be his current primary source of income.

'How long do you think to have her afloat?' A thin mist covered the river beside us as we watched the sunrise over the papyrus. Dop stared silently at the water, drawing on his hand rolled cigarette. Clearly, the longer the cash cow remained, the better.

'Now now or just now?'

'Now now... a month?' Was his opening offer.

'I'll be back in two weeks,' I countered, 'the steering and power are the priority.' I could get the maintenance crew in camp to slap paint on later. Dop didn't reply, I took that to be a general agreement of terms.

As it happened, when I returned with Gypsy to collect The Black Crake, Dop was behind on a few essential tasks. Eager to get going for the long journey home, we reversed out into the river and the helm didn't respond. The wheel span and we drifted out of control into the reed bed as Dop watched from the opposite bank. He had neglected to bolt the final linkages together which did make us wonder what else he might

Shambolic

have missed. That original promise of a different kind of boat came to mind. Dop remained poker faced as we finally got the houseboat pointed downstream and began the voyage to more familiar waters.

From the vantage point of the upper deck I could see the edge of the village. Dop's daughter was leading a donkey with two small children balanced bareback, they were all laughing about something. Perspective is everything.

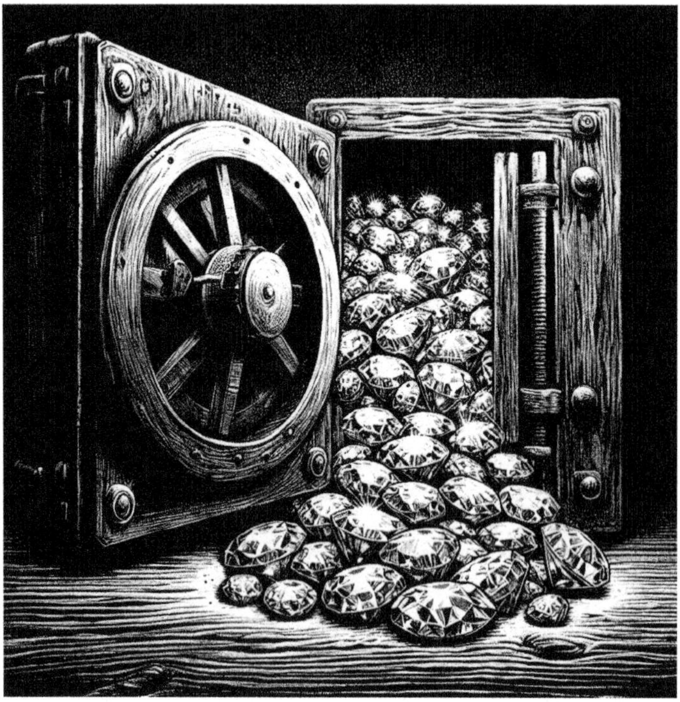

Diamonds Aren't Forever

On a rare visit to Maun, a colleague in camp had asked me to hand deliver a gift to his uncle. Apparently, the easiest way to find him was at the quarry, where he operated the crusher. It wasn't high on my Friday afternoon 'must see' list, but the consequences of that day were potentially transformative.

The uncle was pleased with his gift and insisted on giving me a tour of the establishment in reward. Although I had a couple of mates waiting for me at a riverside bar, I didn't want to appear rude. I won't elaborate on the finer details but there were vast machines chewing through boulders, even larger machines moving piles of rock about the place and all the dust you could dream of.

Despite my best intentions, I began to lose focus until we walked past a pile of stones that caught my eye. They had been separated from the main slag heaps and glinted softly in the sun.

'What are these?' I asked my guide.

'Diamonds.' He said without interest.

'Diamonds!' I stopped dead and, like millions of humans before me, allowed that single word to fill my head with fantasies of huge wealth.

'You can just leave them lying around?'

'These are just industrial grade for cutting tools.'

My original excitement plummeted.

'I lock the precious ones in the safe.'

My interest in local geology ramped back up to lottery winner levels.

'Any chance I could take a look at that?'

I tried to make my request sound casual rather than desperately greedy.

'Sure, let's go to the office.'

Uncle Crusher was obviously used to people asking this when they came to visit.

The office was a metal shipping container that had a breeze block wall built around it. In the centre of the room was a huge safe with chunky dials and a long, metal locking arm. My guide hunched over the dials, so I couldn't see what numbers he was clicking in, and then swung the door wide open. The interior space was filled with metal trays, neatly stacked and numbered with some sort of code, which I assumed meant different grades of stone. I had a clear mental image of Gollum from *The Lord of the Rings* as I craned my head to get a better look.

'Sit at the desk and I'll bring some over.' Uncle said over his shoulder.

I pulled out the wooden desk chair whilst a wide tray was placed in front of me. There were probably two hundred stones of various sizes, all uncut but you could see the potential from the edges that had been cleaned of encasing stone in the quarry process.

'These come from a different area than the industrial standard.'

'So these are real jewellery store diamonds?'

It seemed impossible they'd just be sitting around in this dusty crusher's yard in Botswana.

'These are still low quality, the best stones are at Orapa and they have security like Fort Knox.'

He was clearly enjoying my amateur's reaction to his little chest of treasures.

'Some of them are good enough for those high street shops, mass production places.'

I gazed at his diminutive rock garden and wondered at the collective value.

'You want to take some?'

Seriously, what would you say if someone offered you a pile of ultra precious gems?

'Go ahead and take some, you can enjoy them anywhere in Botswana.'

'Really?' I looked at his face for signs of a trap and considered his apparent geographical restriction.

'What do you mean anywhere in Botswana?'

'You can't take them across the border, they'll lock you up and throw away the key!'

He let out a low whistle to emphasize how terrible that fate would be. Still, how often does someone say you can help yourself to some of Botswana's most valuable exports?

I thought my friends would get a kick out of them in camp, plus, they were free diamonds! My host picked out twenty of the best stones which he then put into a clear plastic bag. The rest of the tour was a waste of time, I had my hand in my pocket, gently stroking my future.

'Are you really that bored of freedom?' Ian stated the obvious. I was sharing some drinks with a couple of pilot friends and had mentioned the diamonds.

'Careful with those my friend,' said Nev, 'they don't fuck around with diamond smuggling here.'

'These are like the floor sweepings though?' I reasoned, mostly to myself.

'They are diamonds that belong to Botswana and DeBeers.' Continued Nev through a puff of cigarette smoke.

'Nev's right, the quality doesn't mean a thing. They love to make big examples of smugglers to deter the next dumb bugger.'

Ian was one of the most volatile drinkers in town and yet here he was handing out sensible advice to his mates.

'I'll keep them at camp to give the punters a thrill.'

I felt like shutting the conversation down, it was spoiling my high as an accidental diamond prospector. In truth, all I could think about was finding a back street stone cutter in Johannesburg to convert my humble chunks of stone into dazzling wealth.

'Hmmm.' Nev caught my eye over the many beer bottles between us. Nev the Hev (short for heavy) was an ex-SAAF combat helicopter pilot, what did he know about taking risks? I kept my head down and my hand in my pocket.

Two months later, my leave cycle came around and, as I started to ponder my travel options, the stones popped back into my head. Once more, like that tortured soul Gollum, they were calling to me, whispering sweet maybes.

'Restore us to glory! Indulge your good fortune! Imagine telling your future bride how her wedding ring came to life in this African adventure...'

'Gollum? What are you talking about man?'

I'd started doing an impression of Gollum out loud and forgotten that the camp manager, Gypsy, was sitting behind me tying flies.

Considering the very human temptation I was debating internally, he was just the man to consult. Gypsy had spent a considerable amount of his youth on the wrong side of the tracks in the South African Cape. He had many juvenile close shave tales to match his skinful of random ink. Gypsy always explained that to raise a few rand as a kid, he allowed the neighbourhood tattoo artists to practice on him. At the end of the day, you make your own luck. He had survived that life and found peace in the great wilderness of Botswana.

'I'm out of here tomorrow and I'm thinking about what to do with these diamonds.'

'Leave them here, bru,' was his assessment and, given his background, he probably knew best.

'It isn't worth the risk and what exactly are you going to do with them in South Africa?'

'Find some jeweller who doesn't ask questions.'

'What if you pick the wrong one and he wants to score brownie points with the cops, he'll just drop you in the shit.'

He had a point, I also didn't have a clue how to find this stonecutter in the first place.

'Yeah, you are probably right,' was my parting comment as I left the office to start packing my kit bag.

That evening I took a couple of American guests out to a beautiful flood plain the locals had named Paradise Flats. The water cover that year was low and the outboard prop skimmed the sandy bottom of the channel, occasionally churning up a cloud of silt but the view was worth the wear and tear. The water sparkled under a fading red sun and herds of Red Lechwe waded between palm islands. A local in his wooden mokoro poled along in the distance; Botswana at its very best. I found a safe island and left my guests to enjoy this majesty alone. As always, the night before I left the Okavango, I was torn between needing a break from the relentless guiding schedule and not wanting to miss a thing in this natural Eden.

My flight into Maun was early the following morning, from there I was driving a borrowed Land Rover to Johannesburg. On my way to the camp's jetty I dropped into the office to grab my passport from the safe. As the safe door swung open, the sunlight caught the corner of my clear plastic bag of uncut diamonds.

'Preciousss! My Preciousss!' Whispered Gollum in his fevered lisp.

Walking down to the boat I had one hand in my pocket, stroking my future, I'd just begun my smuggling career.

It is probably worth mentioning that I was not making this trip alone but with my Austrian girlfriend, Silvia. She knew absolutely nothing about the diamonds joining us for a holiday. Having never driven to Johannesburg before, Silvia was most excited about seeing some new towns and landscape on the way. The route south through Botswana is actually deathly dull, a flat dry landscape with only the occasional stand of trees to liven the view. Small clusters of huts popped up from time to time. Troops of baboons or the odd warthog dashed across the road in front of us. The dominant wildlife along the route was the standard issue African donkey, usually hobbled to stop them escaping to a better life somewhere. The hours ticked by as we passed the towns of Gweta, Nata, Francistown and the capital city of Gaborone.

Our destination was the border crossing at Kopfontein which in my head translated as a *Fountain of Cops* or a *Spring of Law Enforcement*. I'd given the practical issues of diamond smuggling some serious consideration and decided that, if the cops couldn't see them or hear them, they would be undetectable. Keep in mind that African border cops typically like to open boxes and look at the top layer of the contents or pick a container up and give it a good shake. I had solved this problem by pouring my precious treasure into a four-rand bottle of shampoo. No rattle and, unless you drained the goop through a sieve, nothing to see either. Genius!

Now, due to the low speed of the vehicle and a late start from Maun, we arrived just after the border post closed. This was something of an anticlimax as my nervous tension had been rising with every kilometre since Gaborone. I'd run through various scenarios in my head. The best-case scenario was a very busy crossing point, lots of cargo-laden trucks for the police to climb. Maybe a bus or two of economic migrants heading south to find work, they always picked through their paperwork with a tooth comb. Folks like us just drift through in the background on days like that. Worst case, we would be the only vehicle and the bored cops would decide to take the car to pieces panel by panel until finally the contraband was discovered and I was marched at gunpoint to the nearest, mankiest prison cell.

So, to arrive in a highly-strung state and see the border offices locked and the traffic control booms bolted down was a kick in the guts. We had to drive back along the road to a campsite used by the overland groups that frequent the main roads of Africa, pretending they are on safari. The campsite was almost full with various versions of the low budget traveller tribe. The elderly ladies making the most of their dwindling pensions. A few family groups who should have known better than to join the smellies on tour. The majority were grubby young men and women sporting dreadlocks, sunburn and ankle bracelets, plus a few tired looking overland guides.

We found a corner away from the masses and set up camp for the night. I can't say I slept very well, but I wanted to be over the border and out of my misery as fast as possible. I packed the vehicle up whilst Silvia had a quick shower. Then, fully committed, we followed one of the overland trucks down the hill and into the border crossing. As forty or so grubbies began to clog up the various immigration desks, I casually pushed our passports across the counter in the midst of the mayhem. The official didn't even look up as she stamped them both and flicked them back to me. Outside there was no one paying any interest in our Land Rover and I began to relax. We drove the short stretch across the

South African side and here, a cop walked over and waved me to a stop. My pulse rose but I'd prepped for this as well. My standard approach to border crossings was to have some nice-looking treats on open display and share on request. I had a cooler box open on the front seat with iced cokes and biltong on show.

The cop asked where we were coming from, the reason for our trip.

'That is nice looking Botswana biltong my friend, much better than our local stuff...'

I smiled just like a regular tourist and offered him the pack and reached across to include a coke in my small bribe. Heck, I could afford it! He retreated happily to his sentry box and waved us along to the main building where we were stamped through just as easily as before. It wasn't long before the crossing point was receding in the rear view mirror in a cloud of gravel dust.

Too easy, I was starting to see what Al Capone et al were all so pleased about. I felt like a modern-day pirate, master of my own destiny, bending the rules because that's what mavericks do. I had cruised right through the border, flaunting one of the biggest laws in the country and I was untouchable. I couldn't keep my secret any longer so I pulled into the side of the road and told Silvia that I had a surprise she was going to love. She sat in baffled silence as I started searching through our luggage. After ten minutes the roadside was covered in the contents of our three bags.

'What are you looking for, schatzi?'

'The bottle,' I muttered, 'the shampoo bottle.'

'Oh...' she said, 'I'll just buy another one later.'

I stopped my search and looked up.

'Why do we need another one? I want to show you the one I had this morning.'

I wasn't joining the dots just yet.

'I had a shower and I couldn't find mine so I borrowed yours. All those poor overlanders were waiting for showers so I thought I'd just leave the bottle to try and clean a few of them up.'

That was perfectly in character, she was a truly thoughtful person.

I sat down amongst the clothes and books on the ground and considered driving back through the border. That wouldn't look too suspicious,

Shambolic

would it?

'I just want to nip back and collect a bottle of shampoo officer, it's my favourite brand you see...'

I had a vision of some dreadlocked hippy reaching the bottom of the bottle and pouring out a handful of diamonds. He wouldn't know what they were, gooey little bits of stone, some prankster on the bus messing around with the shower kit.

Slumped by the roadside, I had no way to reply verbally to this turn of fortune. Hero to zero in record time. By the time we reached Jo'burg, I had relayed the entire sorry saga to my unwitting accomplice and listened to a well-reasoned argument that getting rid of the bottle was the best thing that could have happened. I do sometimes wonder what further adventures my diamonds and I might have had in South Africa but suspect, on balance, that she was right.

It may be a great song but, in my experience, diamonds aren't necessarily forever.

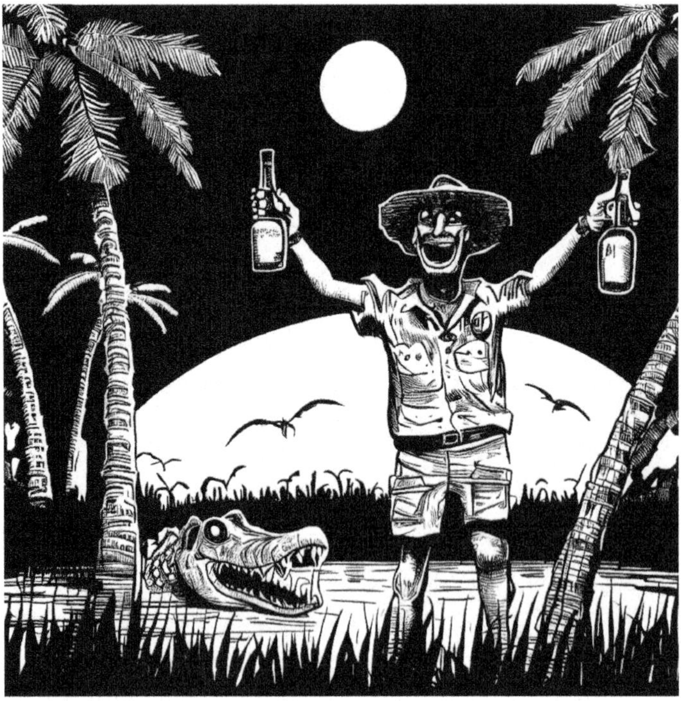

Okavango Crocodile Dundee

When you live in a micro-community of four, the typical number of managers at a small safari camp, any number of additional visitors starts to feel like a party. Once in a while, you enjoy a camp empty of paying guests and a social world enhanced by some transient staff. You can't afford to be particular about your drinking partners on nights like this; pilots, freelance guides, mechanics. If they can tell a story, they add some value.

So it was that one fine night in the Okavango we were a small group gathered around the campfire. The local camp staff enjoying a rare night off at the nearby village amongst family and friends. There were steaks on the grill, foil-wrapped potatoes in the fire and the bar had been open since the sun passed its zenith. Most of our motley crew were feeling pretty clever by the time dinner was inhaled between enough glasses of wine to impress the ancient Romans.

A small scorpion had tumbled from one of the logs on the fire and immediately became the focus for a game of drunken bravado. Dig your foot slowly into the deep river sand and then lift like a soft tectonic plate beneath the pale arachnid. Once in place, how far will you let the critter crawl up your feet before you flick him off to the next reveller? Enthralling as our venomous visitor was, the evening was interrupted by a glorious star fall.

The ground around us was suddenly bathed in a dazzling blast of light. The shadows of leaves projected onto the pale sand at our feet, as the meteorite descended like an illumination flare. Momentary silence fell as we collectively marvelled at the brief, blinding display.

'Shit!'

Someone concisely summed up the general consensus. All the language at our disposal failing to match the moment, the story of our species. Then the bottle came round again and we moved on.

'Hey, Gypsy,' our overnighting aviator, a young South African, spoke up, 'tell us about the fisherman.'

'What fisherman?' asked Silvia, who had just returned from a trip home to Austria.

'A local guy from the village,' Gypsy flicked his thumb in the general direction of Jao village. 'Went missing a few weeks ago. He set out with his fishing net in a mokoro and never came home. Everybody was out searching but we couldn't find a thing, not even the mokoro.'

'What was the deal with the trainers?' interrupted the pilot.

'Trainer,' I corrected, 'just the one.'

'Right,' continued Gypsy, 'so it's been a few days and still nothing. His family don't know what to do, everybody's pretty upset. We had an airport run to do, some clients flying out and we needed to collect a boat we had left in the village. Ben is on the tiller as we head down the channel and then I spot it.'

'Spot what?' asked Silvia, by now everybody is leaning in to hear the full story, the fifth time for most of them.

'Gypsy starts talking about sitatunga,' I pick up the loose end. If you are going to tell a story, better get all the details covered. 'We come around that wide bend downstream and Gypsy starts into a lively commentary on the elusive sitatunga. It was unexpected.'

Gypsy had often said that the majesty of the Okavango spoke for itself and let it do just that. He wasn't a guide given to massive commentary.

'He was pointing at the papyrus on the right bank and tells these folks to look closely as it was a very good spot for the most elusive of antelope. The thing is, we never see sitatunga there, ever, it is an antelope free zone.'

Silvia looked baffled by this talk of sitatunga.

'As the guests peer into the reedbeds as directed, I can see Gypsy trying to catch my eye and tipping his head towards the left bank.'

'Man you were slow to catch-on!' Gypsy sits back with his whisky reflecting the fire like a bowl of embers.

'There's a narrow sand bank on that bend and there, half up the beach, is a big croc. Now Gypsy here is literally insisting the guests keep looking into this endless wall of papyrus. Then I see it too, just beyond the croc, a red trainer.'

The baffled expression remains whilst the rest of the party, knowingly, shake heads at the memory.

'There was a leg in the trainer,' the pilot can't resist voicing the gruesome finale.

Silvia's eyes saucered and a hand covered her mouth.

'Just a leg.'

'Poor bloody bastard,' added a visiting overland guide, which was an understatement.

'Yep, the sitatunga side-show made sense then. Somehow, we got round that bend without anyone seeing anything, which was a miracle. I don't know if that croc killed him or he fell out of the mokoro and drowned before the croc found him.'

Either way, it was a bad end.

'Hmmm,' Silvia looked disturbed and turned to study the black mirror surface of the lagoon alongside us.

Our fire pit sat on a parabola of sand which jutted out into the water just feet away. Gypsy wandered over to the bar to collect another bottle of wine and the talk returned to lighter subjects. I looked for the scorpion without success. He was either back under some deadwood or in someone's discarded boots waiting to surprise them.

The moon bathed all of us with its ethereal glow and the fire sent sparks drifting up into the low canopy of branches overhead. There was some talk of hitting the sack, then the usual spirited defence for more drinking and a night without end. Andy, the overland guide, well into a few pints of grape juice said he was going for a swim. I'll admit, despite the story we had just been sharing, that seemed like a pretty reasonable thing to do on a hot Delta night. Despite a few clearer heads voicing their concerns, I was too drunk to offer a voice of reason. Andy wandered away from the ring of fire light and waded into the shallow water behind us. The wine came around again and I was topping off my glass when the chatter was interrupted by a shout of accusatory annoyance from the dark.

'Who threw a fucking stick?'

It was the night swimmer, wading unsteadily back out of the lagoon. He had me there, nobody else had moved from the campfire and I hadn't seen any flying timber.

'It smacked me in the head!'

He returned to the fire with both hands pressed to his face. Despite the poor light, it was clear that blood was dripping from between his fingers and trailing down his bare chest.

The party stopped, everyone stood to inspect the sudden damage and Andy dropped his hands. There were regular puncture wounds down each cheek, pulsing blood like syrup dripping from a warm maple.

'Fuck! You've been bitten by a bloody crocodile!'

It was obvious and impossible at the same time. What were the chances of this encounter and the fact he had walked away from it without a clue? Alcohol, blurring the line between thrilling life and a hazy happy demise. Andy touched his face again, more carefully and briefly considered the situation before reaching for a beer. We were all used to treating minor injuries in remote camps but a crocodile head bite, that was a collective first.

'I'll get the emergency nurse on the radio,' Aukie said as she headed for the office.

It was the middle of the night but we had a 24-hour channel for things like this. Typically, it was reserved for guests with chest pain and other sinister age-related maladies, not so much for hammered staff using themselves as fishing bait. I wasn't sure what the nurse was going to have to offer us but went to grab the massive, well-stocked first aid kit.

The obvious first step was to pour antiseptic into any bloody wound we could see. Even a band of drunks can manage that, despite the patient being slightly agitated by this point. Growing shock, surging adrenaline and the logic-blunting force of alcohol, combined to a general state of confusion.

Later, through the prism of sobriety, it was clear that he'd had a very close shave. Okavango crocodile Dundee had essentially volunteered to put his head into the jaws of death. Luckily, his assailant couldn't get a decent grip on that sweaty melon and let go. If the rows of razor-sharp teeth had clamped onto almost anything else, we would have been collecting body parts to staple back on in the workshop.

Sobering time passed and it seemed unlikely that he would bleed to death. Infection, maybe some interesting scars and a killer hangover were the most immediate threats. The radio was chirping into the night like a demented cicada as the nurse offered medical advice. Wolfman, the office duty manager in Maun, now roused from slumber, wanted to know if we were discussing a client or a staff member. As it was the latter, the episode was downgraded from emergency medi-vac to, 'let's see how he looks in the morning.' There are only so many Florence Nightingales needed at such times, one to pour the patient stiff drinks and another to pour on TCP.

The party broke up. Nobody likes a gate crasher, especially one that tries to eat one of the invited guests.

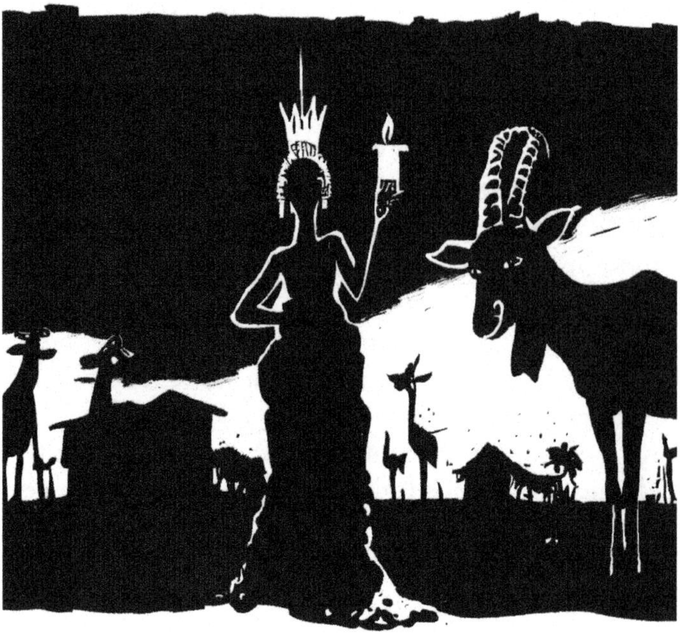

The Jao Beauty Pageant

Having an empty camp for the night usually means the pursuit of simple pleasures for hard working safari folk. Fly-fishing our favourite haunts, cold beer and that rare peak season privilege, unbroken sleep. It just so happened that our night off coincided with a beauty contest in the local village. This was a first, I believe, for both parties. The opportunity to drink anywhere other than at our own bar was a complete novelty so our attendance was pretty much guaranteed.

    A midday flight had carried our last guests away across the Delta. The staff were getting excited and curiously, unveiling clothing that I hadn't imagined they owned. Advocate, our camp hand was, for once, out of his trademark blue overalls. He was sporting a shiny grey suit a la Don Johnson in *Miami Vice*. The Hollywood veneer was shattered, however, when he climbed into his leaky old mokoro and paddled off towards the village.

    Unlike our rakish pathway raker, I didn't have any nightclub finery, just the standard issue khaki uniform that I lived in. Regardless, I was letting the anticipation get to me like some yokel on his first trip to the big city. Flashing lights and amplified disco tunes in the jungle. Jao village was at least two hundred kilometres from the nearest mains power socket, so where would you plug all of this gear in anyway? Exactly how many

Shambolic

AA batteries do you need to power a beauty contest?

Four of us closed shop, which meant locking the office door and flicking the generator off for the night. Motoring away from the totally silent camp was a novelty in itself. We left a couple of storm lanterns on the jetty as our welcome party for later. I could see bats skimming across the lagoon, blurred black shapes appearing briefly in the shallow pools of light. Then the papyrus channel closed in and the island was gone.

On arrival, the village seemed far too quiet to contain something as flamboyant as the extravaganza of loveliness from my imagination. Jao village projected a unique enveloping darkness at night, only coloured by faint candlelight edging a few door frames. All the cooking fires had dwindled to embers, like glowing footprints between the squat huts. It is only tourists who want to sit out marvelling at the stars and silence they have lost at home. A handful of excited children gathered around the one communal structure on the island, a roofless, reed-walled compound used for community meetings and occasional goat storage. The lack of roofing meant that the structure could only be used in the dry season. I suppose mud wrestling competitions might have been an off-season possibility for some local Donald Trump type. There was a sack cloth curtain which doubled as a front door. Beyond this portal I could hear the tinny sounds of the world's cheapest stereo playing UB40 at maximum output.

Whilst we waited in the moonless night for the activities to start, I took photos of the village kids clowning, keen to show off to a new audience. The improv session ended when an olive grass snake joined us and sent the acrobats screaming into the night. Dominance briefly reasserted; the snake slithered on into the gloom. Slowly, Botswana's future leaders drifted back to the compound. Although they had no idea what was going on, like all kids, they were attracted to the source of any commotion. Every time one of them attempted to peek behind the curtain, a hand would appear from the gloom and deliver a hefty slap to the curious face. This routine persisted long enough for us to wonder if there was anything behind the curtain except UB40 and an aggressive hand.

Time passed, the kids tired of getting slapped and wandered home.

Then, with a sudden flourish, the curtain was twitched aside and the hand beckoned us forwards. As the only non-resident attendees, we were given the best seats in the house, on an upturned mokoro. In Paris, this is where the under-fed, coked-up movie stars would sit during fashion week. The lighting engineer had opted for dramatic minimalism. One single candle set in the middle of the stage, with a second burning on the judges' table. The three judges themselves looked totally disinterested as they squinted at each other in the gloom. To my surprise, the head judge was our camp chef. She was a real monster in the kitchen, and, I imagined, a stern referee of beauty contestants. Her fellow pundits were senior members of the community. That tired old motif, *those who can't do, teach*, certainly applied to this particular panel of leathery experts.

As my eyes adjusted to the half-light, it became evident that the contestants were all crammed behind another curtain pinned up in the corner. Nobody seemed to be concerned about their welfare in the stifling evening heat; beauty pageants are a cruel arena indeed. The panel of experts was becoming increasingly argumentative with each other and one of them kept pointing at the ghetto blaster and then the open roof. The contestants only had seconds worth of oxygen left under their heavy curtain. The boma slowly began to fill with village gossips, local posers and several desperate looking older men. That last group were rubbing their thighs and staring at the bulges in the blanket. I won't say it felt entirely tacky but there was a definite cattle-market mood in certain quarters of the room.

The buzz of conversation was interrupted by the arrival of a large woman dressed much like a Christmas decoration. There were glittery ruffles and ostentatious bows liberally strewn about her person. She blew a whistle and delivered a short, harsh speech in Tswana that had everyone peering at her with great expectation. This festive MC stood with one hand on her hip and the other twirling the whistle, a cross between a hooker and a gym teacher. For the benefit of the expatriates, she pointed at the curtain and barked, 'Girls, start now!'

The stereo was cranked up, its thin plastic body vibrating under the internal pressure. Then, finally, the curtain was pulled aside. A line of young women shuffled out into the candlelight to begin something of a funeral march. This was done to the hopeful strains of UB40's 'Cherry oh baby!' They took two bleak laps of the stage before shuffling back under cover. None of the pageant hopefuls had looked up to engage with their audience but had stared fixedly at the heels of the girl in front. This was a very serious affair. Someone at the back of the room clapped a couple of times but stopped when they realised they were the lone cheerleader.

'Now the ladies will walk around one at a time,' said the MC who looked like she was itching to blow the whistle again.

'Start!' she commanded with a roar that drowned out the reggae and had everyone sit bolt upright in alarm. The first solo artist was shoved out from behind the curtain and introduced as Sarafina. She looked to be about twelve and she shuffled very slowly to the reggae. The judging trio began scribbling notes, appraising her with the severity of hawks above a baby rabbit. The old man sitting next to me looked miserable as she trudged past him. Perhaps he wasn't looking for a child bride and had stumbled in here whilst looking for a chess tournament? Regardless, it looked like angst was considered a true gauge of beauty by these girls. The second contestant was somewhat more mature and introduced as Dolly Parton. There was no obvious likeness to the structurally improbable country legend. Dolly shuffled even more slowly than Sarafina and I began to wonder how long this would all take and why, exactly, everyone was shambling at this pace.

The flighty MC was engaged in a heated discussion with a member of the audience. Hands were flapping, voices were raised and the whistle spun on its long cord like a Spitfire prop. Their debate concluded, she strode back to the stage area and announced herself with a loud blast on the klaxon. We all sat up, blasted back to our school days.

'It has been suggested that the girls are not walking properly,' she boomed, 'and someone who is better than them should show them how to walk!'

This was a damning judgement and delivered without concern for the emotional wellbeing of the contestants.

We heard that our head guide had paid twenty-five thebe for the privilege of showing the beauty queens how things should be done on the catwalk. He had wasted his money as his demonstration resembled a constipated child running sideways. The interloper retreated whilst the air filled with hoots of derision. Evidently, if you were prepared to pay hard cash, you could interrupt the proceedings with any old nonsense. Quinton, the camp's relief manager, borrowed fifty thebe from someone and started mincing around the venue in an elaborate catwalk style which went down very well. The old guy looked a little afraid as Quinton took off his shirt and sashayed past with hips swinging. This dark horse entry, like a new flame in the literal darkness, really grabbed the judges' attention. They began writing on their sheets of paper with gusto, this new style was going to score big with the panel of experts.

Girl number three made her entrance and was introduced as Gerard but I suspect that whatever she had told the judges to call her, they were mispronouncing. She added the odd flourish to her shuffle, realising the audience had complex tastes, but was clearly not going to break with tradition at this point. Some of the younger audience members were now dancing in the corners, oblivious to the pageant. This didn't seem to bother the judging panel who, by now, had also stopped paying attention. The old boy next to me was watching the dancers and tapping his foot, this was obviously more his kind of entertainment. Before a full-blown disco could break out, the whistle was blown once again.

Our village matriarch shrilled, 'It has been suggested that the music is too quiet,' many murmurs of agreement in the room, 'and a bigger stereo should be found so that the people can better satisfy their needs!'

No-one mentioned the fact that there was only one candle and it was almost impossible to see the girls anyway. I could have put a billy goat into the contest and won. All I would have to do was teach my hollow-horned ruminant to shuffle and we'd be in with a chance!

A replacement boom box arrived and was connected, with great ceremony, to a car battery. It looked a lot like the original stereo which was busy leaving with its disgruntled owner. As contestant number four began her shuffle routine, the replacement stereo was still silent. She soldiered on regardless, a real professional by anyone's standards. That first lap of the room was completed in absolute silence, without her once losing that signature Jao-shuffle style.

There were shouts for the DJ, then some discussion as to who the

DJ was, before someone finally turned the music back on to rapturous applause. It was too late for contestant number four who wasn't shuffling anymore, she was back behind the curtain. I imagined it was a magic curtain, a gateway that led to some alternative void filled with beauty pageant contestants waiting their turn. The bulges in the limp screen suggested otherwise.

As village pin-up number five appeared, the disco that had been threatening all night finally broke out. The MC, rather than force some sort of order back into the room, boomed that the contest was over and the party was starting. Unlucky contestant number five shuffled on regardless of the dancing that had broken out around her. She limped on, proudly determined in the face of adversity.

We left at that point, the chance of any award ceremony, speeches or dramatic split-decision shuffle-offs were long gone. The flouncy compère was dancing with Don Johnson from our maintenance team, the whistle stuffed into the depths of her cleavage. The old boy who had been sitting next to me was doing a shaky military march with a primary school student. Later we found out that Sarafina had won and the girls were arranging a repeat performance, I suppose to check on the consistency of the judging panel. I'm putting my money on the four-legged challenger with the beard and hooves.

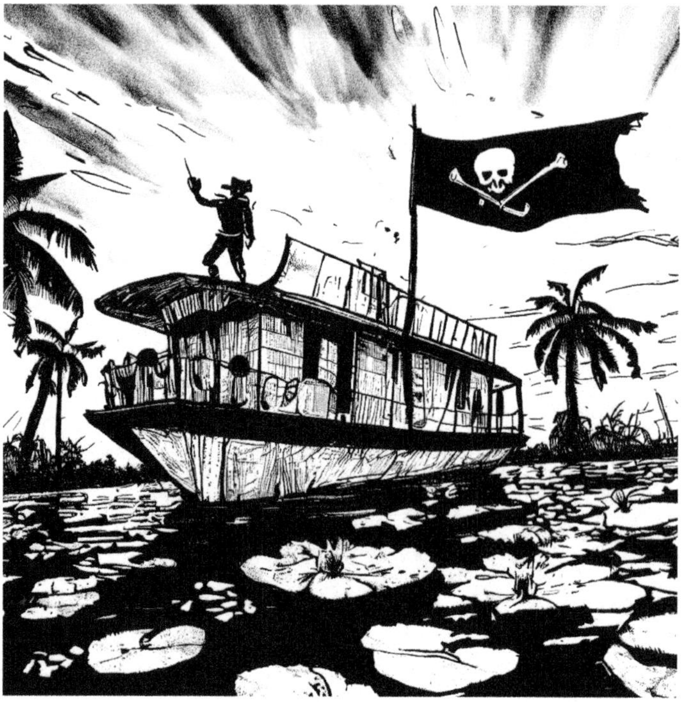

Pirates of the Kalahari

In the mid '90s, some inspired fellow had built a fancy houseboat as an alternative to camping along the Okavango River. He had never used it for much more than gentle day-cruising along the wide Okavango River north of that miraculous lush spread of water, the Okavango Delta. The panhandle, as it is known, offers year-round deep water, easy navigation and access by road for anyone wanting to reach the river. It is a sensible location for a houseboat.

A couple of years later, the company I worked for bought the boat as a base for clients wanting the most remote wetland experience in Botswana. Some hours after that transaction, I became the skipper of the Kubu Queen, *Kubu* being the local word for hippo and *queen* to hint perhaps at the regality of cruising Africa's inland waters. Only a monarch would commission what was essentially a floating cocktail bar in the middle of the Kalahari. Despite Donne's popular observation that *no man is an island*, I was apparently about to become one. Suddenly free from the routines of camp life, it felt more like being a pirate than a safari guide.

The vessel wasn't really designed to thread the maze of papyrus-lined capillaries and shallow lagoons that define the Okavango. It had been conceived as a comfortable living space first and a functioning boat second. That didn't stop us from expanding its horizons and I can't deny it was a huge amount of fun driving a floating safari camp around the backwaters of Botswana.

A month into my tenure as river boat captain, my booking sheet informed me that I would be hosting a family of four from the States. This would be the first family I had on the boat. As I considered the realities of having children loose on board, the chances of this being an epic trip seemed slim.

Several systems were malfunctioning on the boat. These were mechanical problems that the original builder could easily have solved with their exact knowledge of the wiring systems and more. However, I wasn't blessed with that insight. All I knew was that the fans in cabin two had stopped spinning and the solar freezer wasn't freezing. In addition, the hull observation portholes had a disturbing habit of popping out to allow river water to flood the cavity below deck. Pumping large volumes of water from the bilges made even the least observant guests question their safety. The boat builder had told me the vessel was unsinkable thanks to his cunning design which combined three separate hull sections, each filled with sealed bottles. Air trapped inside a void filled with more air. It made sense on paper, a bit like the design of *The Titanic* with its futuristic flood barriers. We all know how that one ended. As for the human element, Hilda, the Scandinavian chef-hostess was on her first Delta voyage. This press-ganged caterer hadn't been too shy to explain that this role was temporary until she could find a position in a 'proper camp', as she described it. Mutinous crew and dubious equipment, situation normal, basically.

The houseboat was moored at the junction of the broad Okavango channel and the Boro River. Jao Island airstrip was located more than an hour down that twisting tributary, easy to blast along in a nimble tender boat. I left my Viking friend cursing over her labours in the cramped galley and hauled a drink laden cooler box to the narrow aft deck. The tender was tied neatly to the stern for easy hauling. Compared to the ponderous double decker, it was like driving a Ferrari. After stepping aboard and casting off, the current quickly pulled the light aluminium boat towards the narrow tributary.

Ben Forbes

The mothership disappeared from view around a sharp papyrus-lined bend in the river and I suffered one of those bad-karma sensations. Turning the ignition key resulted in nothing more than a feeble electronic chirp, not the throaty roar of the 55 hp outboard barking into life. My second attempt didn't even coax a repeat chirp from the engine, just a terminal sounding buzz. The same sound you hear in chip shops when a fly goes kamikaze on the grubby blue neon insect trap. I had now drifted at least half a kilometre from the Kubu Queen. The odds of arriving in time to meet my clients, which is customary practice, were fully diminished.

One problem at a time, that is how you get through the day. I know as much about electronic equipment repair as an Inuit child knows about skydiving. Removing the engine cover to jiggle the neat wiring and tap the polished metal components failed to deliver a solution. The strong current at least pushed me towards my goal as I radioed the camp for a rescue boat. It would take at least thirty minutes for the cavalry to arrive, so I reclined in the bottom of the boat and had a smoke whilst phrasing plausible excuses for my irate clients. I was weighing up the pros and cons of an exciting fiction involving a missionary and a rogue band of hungry pygmies when I spotted a disconnected fuse under the helm mounting. Sometimes, lying back and doing nothing much can lead you to the solution for your problem; new age types call this meditation.

Shortly, as I drifted onto the pale sandy shore of Jao Island, I was rewarded with the familiar drone of a light aircraft approaching over the swamp. The motley crew of hired help at the airstrip were at full attention and ready for action. Johannes, the lead Donkey Deceptor, was draped over a fallen tree like a stoned chameleon. Jackson, the airport manager, reclined in a wheelbarrow, having his head groomed by a small, toothless boy. The boy delivered a wide gummy grin before returning his focus to Jackson's buzz cut.

The sound of the approaching aircraft seemed to lull Johannes into an even deeper and more content siesta. He reminded me of all the cricket matches I had dozed through at school listening to the soporific buzz of bees. The reason for employing this duo was to make sure the airstrip was clear of animals when an aircraft lands and, theoretically, when it takes off as well. Looking beyond the comatose ground crew I counted three donkeys, roughly twenty goats and a small child in a bucket, all in the direct line of the approaching propeller.

There was a whistle hanging at the end of the jetty reserved for situations just like this. I blew it emphatically. Jackson leapt from his wheelbarrow, gathered his wits and ran flailing down the airstrip. It was an impressive sight, pandemonium as a performance art. The result was immediate, the animals scattered, albeit only to the other end of the dusty airstrip. The child fell out of his bucket in terror and crawled to the safety of a nearby russet bushwillow. Johannes hadn't lifted his head once throughout the entertainment, so I dropped my cigarette down the back of his boot. He delivered a stunning recreation of Jackson's charge, but with only one leg. After twenty metres he halted to fish the smouldering Chesterfield from his footwear and puffed happily on the unexpected gift. We were ready to receive our clients who had no idea what sort of people they were dealing with.

It is ancient safari practice to judge a pilot's landing by the number of bounces their craft makes on meeting the airstrip. That and whether or not they hit any large objects like trees. This particular pilot did an admirable job with only a couple of small bounces and no collisions. Impressive, considering the target rich environment offered by the local donkey population. As the Cessna 206 came to a halt in the sand, I caught a glimpse of a perm hairdo and one of those sun visors favoured by roulette croupiers. The pilot climbed out and gave an almost imperceptible shake of the head. A warning? I looked over his shoulder to assess the incoming damage.

The patriarch was first out of the Cessna. He had the pilot's seat belt wrapped around his ankles which tripped him headfirst into the sand. To compensate for this unfortunate slapstick dismount, he stood up rapidly and banged his head into the underside of the aircraft wing with a dull metallic thud. The pilot removed his sunglasses to inspect the small, perfectly round imprint of a human skull in the flexible bodywork. Johannes giggled and I stepped forward to fill the awkward silence with a welcome handshake. I knew my client's name was Doug because it was on the booking sheet and was also helpfully embroidered onto his polo shirt.

'Hello, Doug, welcome to Jao.'

'Terminal Three!' added Jackson smartly which received a puzzled frown from our guest.

I didn't have the chance to elaborate because Doug was shoved aside as his wife exited the aircraft. Resplendent in gold jewellery and several layers of leopard print material, she would have attracted admiring glances from would-be muggers anywhere on the planet. My first thought was that she might become a target for poachers.

'I'm *Chrystal!*' the name was enunciated quite slowly, as if we were deaf or simple, 'will we be in any danger?'

As introductions go, this was a first for me and I suspected that their travel agent had been rather vague when briefing their client. I began to form a reassuring response, but Chrystal turned away to summon the remaining self-loading cargo from the cramped interior of the air taxi. Doug had wandered across to watch the pilot unload their luggage from the pod riveted to the undercarriage. Chrystal clucked as she inspected her children, unscathed after the fifty-minute flight from Maun. Jackson looked at me in genuine amazement as I considered the relatively small space we would all be sharing for a few days.

Our little group grew as the two boys joined us. The youngest was a hyperactive looking child introduced as Brad, accompanied by his elder brother, KG, who stared hard at my feet. This turned out to be something of a default setting for son number one. Had they been modern art, they'd have been called something like 'Chaos and Density pt.2.' Johannes gathered some luggage and began walking towards the boat station with Brad on his heels. Jackson kicked a large, wheeled suitcase as if he was checking the pressure on a car tyre, shook his head and hauled it across the sand leaving a pair of deep furrows. A very basic rule of small aircraft travel is to pack light and use soft luggage so the pilot has a fighting chance of squeezing everything into his bijou freight space. In the complicated dating game of client and destination, I wondered if this family might have been directed to the wrong continent. Regardless, the burden of delivering an unforgettable experience whilst imparting my knowledge of the fascinating flora and fauna fell to me;

so it said, in my contract.

After loading both luggage and family into the tender, we heard the aircraft blast down the strip and slowly fade into the distance. Jackson pushed us off the bank and the papyrus closed in on the small boat. Doug turned from watching the speck of an aircraft and stated, 'We're from LA so we're used to the jungle!'

I wasn't convinced that he meant it as he warily glanced around. I put that down to first day nerves and remained optimistic that I could awaken their frontier spirit. The boys had given up on the call of the wild and were engrossed in their matching Nintendos. I'll be honest and admit that children were a mystery to me at that point in my life. I knew they needed sugar and TV to function but I had no idea how you made them appreciate the majesty of the natural world. Our journey up river passed in hushed apprehension as the Okavango overwhelmed the group with its ethereal beauty. Pointing at an impressively manicured talon of an adult fish eagle, Chrystal asked, 'Is that at all dangerous?'

'Only if you are a fish,' I replied honestly.

Then, the Kubu Queen swung into view, exactly where I hoped it would still be. I was reminded just how small my floating safari camp actually was when faced with the children. Brad thought it looked cool until I admitted there wasn't a television. To sprinkle some icing on the moment, Hilda the Viking had decided to spend her down-time sunbathing and she put her khaki uniform shirt back on a little too slowly to retain her full dignity. Doug looked surprised, Chrystal frowned and the boys, looking at their screens, missed the sighting altogether.

The contents of the tender boat happily spread themselves out across the upper deck of the houseboat on the long sofas and hammock. I armed them all with an ice-cold drink in preparation for their safety briefing. Brad provided a practical illustration by getting a *Mepps* fishing spinner hooked through his elbow. Doug asked me what time they would be leaving for the next camp. You can't take this sort of thing personally; if you roll the client dice often enough, eventually you come up snake eyes. The only person paying any attention to my briefing was Chrystal, highly risk-aware and borderline hostile to the wonderful possibilities of the African bush. She had a great many safety concerns and asked me if any large reptiles had ever clambered aboard the boat. I was pretty sure I could arrange it if there were no witnesses.

Whilst I was offering reassurance to mother, father was embroiled in parenting duties. A fight had broken out between the boys and Brad had been dispatched to his cabin as punishment for some act of fraternal torment. The cabins were about two metres by one and as likely to keep a twitchy juvenile contained as Hilda was to sign up for the next voyage of discovery. Almost immediately the cabin door slammed shut, the unrepentant child climbed out of the wide window and loitered noisily on the engine deck at the back of the vessel. A hush descended on the upper deck as we all waited to see how Doug was going to handle this act of disobedience. He picked up a copy of *National Geographic* and disappeared uneasily into its glossy pages. Chrystal remained seated at the bar, so I walked to the back of the deck. Leaning over the railing I tapped the varnished wood until Brad glanced up.

'Crocodiles,' I pointed at the dark water flowing a foot from Brad's sneakers.

His small head rotated down, back to me and then back to the river. He then shuffled carefully along to his cabin window and disappeared back inside.

The sun had passed its apex which meant we had to get moving. As the twin engines idled, I hauled the anchor free from the thick sediment of the riverbed and coiled the long chain into its metal locker. The skies were a perfect blue as we steamed into the Delta where adventure and a great many mosquitoes awaited us. One of several design quirks onboard the Kubu Queen was the mahogany topped bar being wrapped around the helm. Excellent for alcoholic skippers but a potential problem if you were hoping for some peace whilst navigating the waterways. Bars on boats function like kitchens at parties, they attract people. Curiously, Doug was reading an article on the rich marine life of Fiji. Given our location, that was like sitting in front of a Rembrandt whilst wearing a VR headset tuned to the Bob Ross experience. Chrystal was still with me though and her voice drew my gaze from a jacana stepping masterfully across a carpet of daylilies. I hoped we were going to move into serious discussion of the natural Eden we found ourselves travelling through. I was wrong; she wanted to talk about her children, their hobbies, their grades, their potential. As much as I hoped she would be curious about my world, I was just the facilitator. Cab drivers, barmen and safari guides fulfil one common purpose for their clientele, a non-judgemental ear. On this particular safari, I was all three professions anyway. Her glowing testimony was cut short by the return of son number two who stuck his little melon up the stairwell, pointed overboard and shouted, 'Lookit!'

As we drew level with a break in the papyrus, we all spotted a Red Lechwe, in the last gasp of life with a great chunk missing from its hindquarters. A few feet away in the river lurked an impressive crocodile, at least four metres long, with a bucktail-garnished grin. The unfortunate antelope was slumped onto its front legs and eyeing the great reptile with a look of tired predestination. Doug had flung his magazine aside to grab his camcorder and quickly sizing the situation up, announced, 'I think that deer is sick!'

Tempted as I was to say that this blood loss was a seasonal peculiarity amongst Botswana's antelope species, that would have been unnecessarily cruel. For the second time that day I said, 'Crocodile,' and pointed to the cold-blooded assassin.

Doug peered harder through his viewfinder until he spotted the beast, 'Jesus! You're right, look at the size of that sucker! You see that honey?'

Chrystal's expression was impossible to interpret but she moved to pull her youngest up the steps and away from the railing, lest he should end up in the river and on the menu. KG was still seated on the long couch with his Nintendo and headphones; he reached for his can of Coke, eyes glued to the tiny screen. The crocodile watched the lechwe, the lechwe appeared to shift his gaze to me and I willed encouragement. KG belched, the antelope decided that the afterlife was preferable to the present company and rolled onto its side to die in the warm sand. Wise. The crocodile hauled itself half out of the water to claim its prize and all of us watched silently as he submerged, feet from the port hull.

Doug broke free from the viewfinder and glanced at the deck beneath his feet. I knew what he was thinking, just how thick is that hull?

'Don't worry, he has his meal.'

It looked like he might ask for structural specifics but we were interrupted by Hilda who had kept herself out of sight until now.

'Where is the braai?' It was an accusation rather than a question.

'Braai?'

'The one I asked the camp hand at Juh-deeby to take and clean!'

Like Doug, Hilda was on her very first stint in Africa. As far as I knew, this was her first job in the safari business. So fine, ask the camp hand, a very casual fellow called Advocate, to go and clean the braai. Who knows? He might actually do it. But, to assume he was going to bring it back afterwards? I couldn't see why this was my problem. I didn't want my guests thinking they would have to eat Weetabix for the next three days and deployed that eyebrow raise that Roger Moore relies so heavily on, to convey the message to my angry chef. She continued to smoulder for a few more moments, then turned on her heel to return noisily to the tiny galley. I could imagine her first expletive laden letter home after this trip. Since I was planning on sacking her shortly there would be plenty to write about. We had four superb cooks in camp who came from the nearest village and they could all produce a three-course meal with nothing but hot coals and roadkill. I just had to convince one of them that joining the Botswana Naval Reserve was an excellent career move.

It was still only three in the afternoon and there was no way I could get away with a proper drink unless someone else suggested it first. I had some minimum standards on board, one of them being that the skipper had to be at least as sober as the least intoxicated client.

We cruised upstream until an hour before sunset. Our elevated vantage point provided incredible views across lagoons to the numerous islands dotted off the main channel, each one a tantalising lost world all its own. Egrets and herons stalked the dense papyrus, balancing themselves on branches and the long flexible papyrus stems. Coucals chorused their bubbling song and, in the distant trees, vervet monkeys hunted fruit on the small patches of dry land. We passed an ancient fisherman in a heavily patched mokoro. He had stretched a short nylon net across the entrance to a side channel. A wisp of smoke rose from the island behind him, his camp for the fishing expedition. He would probably set snares to try and catch something bigger than a whiskered barbel. I supposed I

Shambolic

would do the same in his position, nature is a resource. We are naïve to assume everyone can afford to buy into our currently non-consumptive approach to African wildlife.

As we cut on through the mirror-calm river, our wake shimmered like a living watercolour. Doug studied a large map of the Okavango that I had framed and bolted to the wall. He wasn't entirely clear on some geographical matters.

'So we're on the Okavangah River?'

'The Okavan-go, correct.'

'Now, where does the water come from?'

Which was a good question.

'Angola.'

'That's somewhere in Botswana?'

Which wasn't such a good question.

'No, that's a different country, called Angola,' I pointed to the northern border on the map.

'Oh right… are we going there?'

He peered at the map and held his hand up like a measuring tool.

'No, it's a very long way off.'

Vague seemed best. Doug was silent as he considered these pieces of basic information.

'But Botswana is part of South Africa?'

That was the worst question so far.

'No, that's a different country as well but Botswana is part of southern Africa.' It seemed like a compromise, they sound similar.

Now, don't be angry with Doug here because, as much as I appreciated well-briefed clients, Botswana thrived on travellers who were more interested in the wildlife than the specifics of location. African nature just needs enthusiastic ambassadors to care, otherwise everything I loved was at risk. Either way, the geography lesson was over as we arrived at the spot I had planned to overnight, a wide stretch of the river between two small islands. The throttles were in neutral and the big houseboat settled into the current and held steady whilst I dropped the anchor overboard. As the metal claws searched for purchase we drifted back six metres before the chain snapped taut and we swung into mid-channel. I cut the engines from the helm and the full chorus of sunset washed over us.

Baboons chattered from the island ahead while a pod of hippo had a loud discussion in the lagoon beyond the dense papyrus channel boundary. Something made a splash behind us and Brad ran to lean over the stern rail and watch for swamp monsters. As the sky bled from amber to pale red, I turned on the few systems that made life comfortable after dark. Cabin lights and fans (when they worked) and the upstairs communication lights to announce our hulking presence to anyone enjoying a nocturnal speed boat tour, like poachers or the Botswana Defence Force hunting them.

As I did every single evening as the sun fell from our sky, I smelled the breeze and considered our most numerically superior enemy, the indomitable mosquito. If you just flick every light switch on the boat, the single light source for miles around, you can pretty much guarantee squadrons of winged assailants making a buzz line for you.

'Fellas! The party boat is back, mine's a pint of Negative-O please, bar keep!'

There was the lightest of breezes which might help delay the mosquitoes but, as I stared into the gloaming, I heard a series of loud slaps behind me. Young KG had been forced to put his gameboy down to combat some incoming air traffic. He beat at his head a few times and delivered a karate chop to the air. There was a full bottle of *Peaceful Sleep* bug spray three feet away on a low bookcase but sometimes children have to work things out for themselves, don't they? KG ignored his canned saviour and disappeared downstairs to hide in his cabin which, after a long hot day, would have been as refreshing as a sauna. Chrystal had Brad in a half-nelson and was applying a layer of something that smelled of lemons and was going to prove popular with the little critters in our midst.

I told my guests that dinner would be served in an hour and, as often happens, they took this as some sort of dismissal notice. The more upmarket camps are places where a shower and a fresh set of safari-chic finery are pretty much de rigueur but, on the Kubu Queen, I liked to keep things casual. That was because I had a very limited wastewater storage capacity, another serious design flaw.

Ironically, I could pump beautiful river water through a filter and into the shower all day long, I just couldn't dispose of the end product until I returned to camp. A hygiene Catch-22. So I waxed lyrical about the precious resource that water really was in Botswana. I might have laid it on a bit thick with my fictional usage equations, one five-minute shower means a subsistence farmer loses one calf a year. Rather a guilty but rapid minute of hot water than a full septic tank and a closed sign on the door to the head. Strangely, the original owner had fitted a vast fuel tank that could have allowed for a week of exploration. However, he had then decided that six adult humans would only need to flush the toilet twice and share a twenty-four second shower in that time.

In readiness for dinner, I swung the ship's insect distraction light out from its resting place. A two-metre length of tubular metal with a single bright all-weather bulb at the far end. I had seen them used to great effect on Lake Kariba and had borrowed the idea. In theory the brightest light attracts the majority of the bugs; it works some of the time as long as you keep all on-board lighting comparatively dim. The bulb was instantly coated in the good and the great of the Okavango's insect society. They, in turn, attracted that master of stealth aviation, the bat. It was mesmerising to watch, a metal stick with a 10-rand bulb delivering more thrills than your local multiplex. Doug and I were certainly enjoying the show but a shriek from the galley reminded me that I hadn't yet rolled down the canvas blinds to keep the wildlife from disturbing the chef. A muttered stream of vitriol drifted up the stairs and we either learnt the Danish word for *bat* or for something less wholesome.

Chrystal joined us at the bar. She was impressively wrapped in camouflage chiffon, like a wealthy terrorist at a dinner party. I raised an empty glass in invitation and she asked for a straight scotch on the rocks. As chief bartender, I considered taking something down to the Viking but stimulants seemed they might be counterproductive in her unhappy state.

The Kubu Queen was momentarily peaceful as the calm river reflected the crystalline heavens like a celestial Aladdin's cave. We were literally adrift in the milky way, a visual mystery equal to anything that an astronaut might have seen. The only reminder that we were still earthbound was the incessant whine of those winged intruders. That, and the arrival of the children which cracked the fragile peace on the top deck.

'Can I have a beer dad?' implored KG.

'Well...'

Curiously Doug looked at me for some sort of confirmation, perhaps due to my status as official barman. Well, there were no rules about underage drinking on my boat, only rules about conserving septic tank capacity. During our brief time together I had seen their eldest child struggle somewhat with his new surroundings. I wasn't convinced that alcohol was going to be his natural ally but, then again, what damage could a few weak local beers do? Doug grinned and Chrystal rolled her eyes as I poured a glass of St Louis for their first born. This locally brewed light beer has a lower alcohol content than Scottish tap water, so everything was going to be just fine. Proactive Brad was almost inverted as he climbed into the cavernous fridge to search for a can of Coke.

At that moment, Hilda arrived with the first tray of food which she deposited on the bar without comment. I waited to hear what the menu was for the evening, a tradition in all safari camps, floating or otherwise. I was still waiting when the family descended on their starters of gazpacho and freshly baked bread. Hilda crept back downstairs and I joined in the silent feast, making a mental note to supply more bar snacks tomorrow. The steak went the same way and I tried to recall a time when I had seen guests focus on their food with such predatory intent.

Conversation was the one way I could see to avoid some sort of group heartburn calamity and to calm the ravenous family down. Not just any conversation, but one carefully designed to elicit a drowsy response and an early bedtime for the boys. Picture me as the kindly uncle tasked with bedtime stories, a master at soporific storytelling. I introduced them to the wonderful world of termites, a genuinely fascinating insect if you like that sort of thing. I described their typical routines, diet, their excavations for water, their methods of construction, predators, anything that sprang to mind. Brad was asleep before my first deep breath and KG was fidgeting like a dog with worms.

Dinner was gone and I thought I had accomplished my mission when Doug suddenly threw a curve ball.

'A termite is an ant right?'

'An ant?' I had a sinking feeling.

Shambolic

'It's the same as a termite?' Persisted Doug.

'No, a termite isn't an ant, they belong to different insect families, they have different social structures, different diets...'

Even as I spoke I sensed my early-to-bed strategy was unravelling, a complete failure to launch.

'But they are both *very* small aren't they?'

Doug said this somewhat like a TV detective introducing his case-solving evidence.

'Hmmm.'

'So aren't they in the same family, you know the class or whatever?'

'Classification', I corrected, as I reached for the remains of the wine.

'Yep,' he was warming to his theme and a small part of me was happy that he was focussing on nature.

I tried to think of a way to steer Doug away from the idea of a species classification system based on physical size. It had been a long day and I was into the deep end of the merlot.

'A medium sized gorilla is about the same size as a very large man, isn't it?' I ventured though, as I said it, I knew it was a bad example.

'Sure,' Doug didn't give it much thought.

'Well, they are still completely different, aren't they...'

I waited.

'Gorillas have hands!' interjected KG who seemed to have been startled awake.

'We are all primates, but having hands doesn't automatically grant them membership to the human race though, does it?'

'You fellas enjoy yourselves!' said Chrystal as she carried her inert younger son off to his cabin; she knew when a waste of time was in progress.

'Does a gorilla eat ants?' Doug was near the end of a slender branch of the towering tree of biological knowledge.

'Chimps eat termites,' I said, but we had drifted so far from the original topic, I couldn't see the distant shore anymore.

'Could a gorilla kill a crocodile in a fight?' asked the teenager at the table who had veered right into a Marvel comic storyline. He was picturing a gang of apes intercepting a croc at some jungle street corner.

Fortunately for me, Hilda appeared and settled onto the end of the long sofa. I grabbed the opportunity and explained that I needed to check the fuel tanks. There is a narrow deck built around the outboard engines and I sat on top of the starboard Yamaha to enjoy a quiet smoke. From my safe space I could hear the captive chef fielding dozens of questions from a strangely animated KG. Finally he asked her if she had a boyfriend and his father made a quick excuse; I could hear them tramp along the corridor to their cabins and then silence.

If Hilda was disappointed to miss out on that prize catch, she hid it well. By the time I returned to the steering deck, she was cocooned in a sleeping bag. I had told her to use a mosquito net if she wanted a quiet night but instead she was wrapped in a thermal defence shroud. The chink in her nocturnal armour was the small hole through which her face protruded. One of the very many tools in the annoying arsenal carried by mosquitoes is their ability to detect carbon dioxide as we breathe out. We literally blow a flight path for the blood-thirsty little creatures. I could see that the squadron had realised the target area was now smaller than they might prefer, but they were compensating for that with a determined assault on Hilda's rosy cheeks. I hung a spare net from the roof beams and draped it across the top half of my press-ganged assistant, a small gesture of solidarity on what I knew would be our only voyage together.

The boat was as much a part of the night as the water beneath us and the reeds marking the channel. Painted reed frogs stuck to the hull like fridge magnets, great moths explored the corridor and open decks. The crescendo call of a pearl-spotted owl signified an island close by and I floated on the night breeze just like those dark butterflies. Alone with your thoughts, it's a dangerous time when the impossible romance of the African wilderness can fool you.

The River Horse

I fell asleep with a heart full of joy and woke with nostrils full of the devil's codpiece. The stench was so strong that my eyes were watering before I could fully open them. I registered that it was very early morning, the guests were apparently still asleep but a rotten cloud had enveloped our small island of dreams. Whatever the cause of the evil stench, I wasn't going to discover it from beneath my tangled mosquito net.

I crawled to the edge of the deck and squinted down to the waterline. The gentle sweep of the bowline was sporting an additional embellishment, a grotesque figurehead. Four swollen legs stuck up from beneath the water as if we had crashed into a coachman's dray horse. Hippos have comically chubby knees by design, but once they start to bloat with putrid fumes, they look like pantomime props. In the night, a deceased river horse had drifted down the channel and wedged beneath our bow.

I staggered down the steps, wrapping my T-shirt around my face to try and block out the toxic vapours. My brain was misfiring under the olfactory overload and my first desperate attempt to separate boat from beast using a long wooden *ngashi* resulted in an extra hole in the hugely inflated belly. The green slime that fizzed out into the early light of day was a similar colour to the contents of my stomach which went over the side of the boat in an uncontrollable reaction. It was getting grim. I started to imagine my clients clambering from bed and everyone ending up head-down over the stern. Forget the tip on this trip, captain. To make matters worse, the chubby cadaver was wrapped in the anchor chain like a bloated heiress in a set of heavy pearls. We were literally tied together so I did the only thing I could, I released the great shackle that held the chain in place.

The houseboat started to drift downstream and the hippo bobbed in the current like a rancid cork, beginning to roll as the current unwound it from its shackles. Almost immediately, a crocodile took hold of a rear leg and started tugging the entire deflated catastrophe towards the reed bed. I wanted to brush my teeth with bleach and shave my tongue to clean some of the earthly stink away but I had to start the engines before we began bouncing along the riverbank.

Hilda sat upright in alarm at the sound of the outboard engines and I could hear voices grumbling below deck. It was a cruelly early wake-up call but considerably better than the malodorous version of moments before. The Viking appeared at my elbow and sniffed the air, still faintly foetid, as I pointed upstream to the hippo which now hosted two croco-diners.

I still had to regain the fifty metres of anchor chain which were attached to a small buoy I had connected for just such emergency cast-off situations. It meant that I could pick-up the lost chain without having to swim for it, especially useful when the water was coming alive with hungry leviathans. I motored slowly forwards until the buoy was bobbing just in front of the bow, left the helm to dash down the steps, leant overboard and grabbed the chain. Doug wandered along the corridor to see what the noise was all about and watched as I hauled the long chain back into its metal case. The first few metres were fine but then I started to find chunks of slimy hippo flesh slipping between my fingers and considered another tactical chunder. Doug wisely backed away and returned to his cabin, closing the door.

Hilda was becoming anxious about the large vessel motoring without a skipper, an amateur's concern. I suppose in Denmark it is normal to have someone steer a boat under power but, as the only houseboat on the entire river system for several hundred miles, I wasn't worried about a collision. The Kubu Queen chugged gently into the current whilst I poured water from a bucket over the grisly links. There was no way I was going to eat breakfast, possibly ever again. Finally, the evidence was rinsed back into the river and I let the reattached anchor hold us midstream again. The engines fell silent and my clients returned to see what the early start was all about, it was still only six in the morning, after all.

'Apologies for the rude awakening everyone,' I explained, 'we had an unexpected visitor this morning.'

Brad was especially excited when I mentioned the dead hippo and the crocodiles.

'Can we see it?' Doug asked what was clearly on his son's mind.

'Sure,' though I wasn't especially keen to return to the scene myself, 'it doesn't smell too good though!'

I had warned them but this didn't diminish their eager anticipation as the three of us clambered into the tender.

It only took a minute to catch up with the drifting hulk which was shuddering grotesquely as the local dinosaurs ripped chunks from underneath the carcass. On closer inspection, I could see Doug was losing some of his enthusiasm, proximity to ugly realities can do that to people. Brad was thrilled until the wind briefly turned, in stomach-churning happenstance. I left the crocs to their meal as I spun the tender and its retching crew back upstream. Breakfast was going to be a very simple affair. Brad chattered away with the most enthusiasm for the natural world since I had met him. Perhaps the rancid hippo was going to be the catalyst for his appreciation of Botswana's wild riches. Or perhaps he was just a typical kid who couldn't believe he had just seen a crocodile taking chunks out of something.

Hilda prepared a basic breakfast for those who still had the stomach for food and I hauled anchor and got us moving further north. I had to get the family to the nearest airstrip at Seronga village for a late afternoon flight. Chrystal was reading a glossy magazine, KG was plugged back into his Nintendo but I still had father and the spare heir dialled into their surroundings. If I had achieved nothing else on this safari, we had made some small progress towards surface level assimilation. Two hours later we had seen a number of sunbathing crocodiles, a small herd of lechwe on a flood plain and very briefly, a sitatunga, that most elusive of the Delta's antelope species. Sitatunga are unique amongst antelope in their willingness to submerge themselves to avoid land predators.

One possible crocodile versus a pride of lions seemed like a fair balance of risk and reward.

Mugged

'Fancy some fishing Doug?'

'OK,' not entirely enthusiastic, 'do we need bait?'

I sensed that Doug had previous experience of worms on hooks and hadn't enjoyed the experience very much.

'No, we can use spinners,' I pointed to the rods already rigged with shiny little *Mepps* fish magnets. 'You can't go wrong!' which was a lie because no other human endeavour has as much potential for wasting time in tangled frustration as the pursuit of fish.

We moored in a small lagoon which offered the non-fishing crew the best chance of spotting some wildlife. Chrystal told Brad he had to stay on the big boat and I was happy to enforce that wise policy as the tender wasn't big enough for three fishermen. Doug climbed into the small boat and I loaded a cooler box of drinks, a heavy tackle box and two rods.

Planing along the main channel blew away the less pleasant memories of that morning and our immediate horizon filled with possibilities. I'll admit that I'm happily addicted to fishing, my favourite excuse for deserting the houseboat and niggling maintenance duties. A likely looking side channel came into view and, as we surged to a halt, a crocodile submerged. A good omen from the river god. They are the keenest pescatarians in the neighbourhood and their very presence is like a glowing restaurant review.

Doug eyed the rippled surface warily before getting to his feet when I handed him a rod.

'Just remember to keep the line tight, no slack,' I advised, 'otherwise the tiger fish will just bite through and take the spinner with them.'

'These suckers have teeth?' Doug sat down again. 'Are they dangerous if they get in the boat?'

'They aren't dangerous Doug, just fish with little teeth, like a pike. They are predators, they hunt other fish.'

I wasn't sure that my explanation was making my companion any more comfortable but I figured that once we had caught a few fish, he would start to enjoy himself. I had him watch as I made a cast so he knew how the reel worked and then indicated that he should have a go. Doug took a look at the water beside us and cast his shiny silver spinner into a clump of hippo grass. No problem, a warmup cast and we motored over to retrieve his tackle. His second cast arced prettily through the late morning air into the branches of a water fig, where it dangled like a Christmas decoration. This was definitely limiting Doug's chances at catching a fish and I sensed an air of defeat coming over him.

'Try casting straight downstream,' I advised after I had pulled his decoration back from the branches. Then I turned to stare at nothing through my binoculars; sometimes an audience isn't the motivation a nervous caster needs. As I listened I heard the soft whizz of the line leaving the reel and then a satisfying splash as he hit the target. Doug

Shambolic

breathed out in audible relief and I glanced over my shoulder to nod some encouragement, everyone deserves a win now and again.

I didn't have the chance to comment before the line went taught and the reel started screeching. Doug froze and a decent sized tiger fish broke the surface to hurl itself angrily into the air in a bid to shake the spinner loose. It is one of the most glorious experiences in African sport fishing. I'm sure a sailfish breaching at 25 knots is impressive but give me the muscular glitter of the tiger any day. Each dazzling scale looked like a leaf of elven silver beaten and rolled to reflect the sun.

'What now!' yelled Doug in panic.

'Tight line! No Slack!'

Simple instructions to overcome an adversary with a score of possible escape plans. The fragile nylon umbilical was cutting through the surface sheen like a laser when the fish decided to change tack and ricochet back towards us. This was Doug's moment, his time to match the primaeval instincts of this perfect killing machine.

'Reel in! Reel in!'

I was leaning out of the boat to monitor the return run. Doug set about the task with some vigour and I was impressed he almost kept up with his prey.

'I think I've got it!' yelled Doug with the most unguarded enthusiasm I had witnessed since we had met.

Fishing, it rarely fails to light the fire.

'It's still fighting...'

The line went completely slack, the energy vaporised, as suddenly as a fuse blowing or a kite breaking loose in a gale. It was as if the fish had never existed but then the dark green surface revealed a fleeting glimpse of unmistakable prehistoric body armour. Doug gaped and sat down in shock. His first contact with our greatest fighting fish had ended in a blunt reminder of who really controlled these waters.

'If you are going to lose a fish,' I consoled, 'then that is the way to do it!'

I handed Doug a cold beer; this was far from failure as far as I was concerned. Catching our finest fish and then getting mugged by a crocodile, what a pleasure!

'More fish or lunch?' I offered.

'Have you ever seen that before?' Doug was awake to the uniquely African situation we had stumbled into.

'Never,' I lied, because it would make a great story and Doug's kids were going to think he was a mathematically capable version of Quint from *Jaws*.

Nowhere on earth provides such casual possibility to add to your personal legend than wild Africa. The short cruise back to the mother ship was taken in contented silence. Egrets stalked the reed beds, a goliath heron swept across our bow, Doug finished his beer and life was good. Our engine approach had attracted a small audience on the top deck of the Kubu Queen as we pulled alongside.

'You won't believe this!' called the latest convert to the art of fishing. I busied myself with preparing the boat for our final journey as Doug huddled with his family to share his epic tale. I could hear Brad demanding to hear about the size of the crocodile, the size of the fish, the size of the collective teeth, the proximity of all of this to his father. I hoped Doug was laying it on thick as we swung out into the main channel and headed for Seronga airstrip.

An hour later, we were loading ourselves into the tender when the Cessna we were due to rendezvous with buzzed up the river and banked towards the dirt strip. Hilda passed down the last couple of hard-cased bags which reminded me of how much the pilots hated their daily games of luggage *Tetris*. She then surprised us all with a wide smile and a friendly wave as I gunned the small boat after the aircraft. Chrystal was peering at a printed itinerary but Doug was watching the passing scenery. He nudged his eldest son and pointed out a Jacana carefully stepping across a bridge of lily pads.

'Where do they lay their eggs?' he asked me, which was a good question.

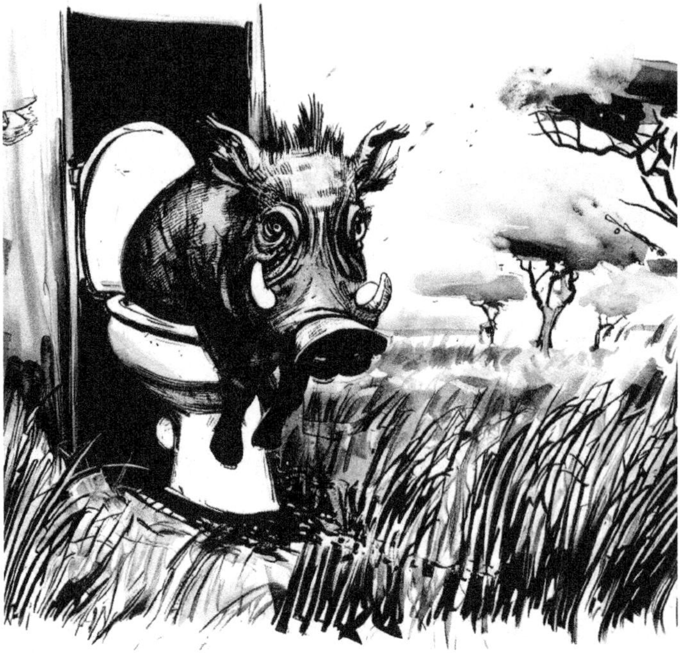

The Most Dangerous Thing in Africa

When asked for his opinion concerning the most dangerous thing in Africa, Ernest Hemingway cynically said 'Women!'

Well, Ernest was wrong because the most dangerous thing in Africa is a septic tank. I will take a charging rhino, demented divorcee or a cornered leopard over these vile necessities any day. In theory, a septic tank and its companion soakaway pit is built, buried and then left alone. The septic tank for a safari tent is a large plastic container about one and a half metres tall by one metre wide. The adjoining soakaway is as big as the available space allows because you never want to have to dig another one. A proper soakaway is filled with stone rubble and other junk then covered in cloth before being buried. You can walk across it quite safely and nothing will happen to you. In most safari camps that I've seen, the deep pit is covered with strips of corrugated tin, sometimes supported with a few mouldy planks. That way, you can walk over the top and have a better than average chance of falling straight in. It pays dividends to know the locations of all these tank traps in your camp.

Now throw in the wildcard of nature and you end up with elephants, hippos, visiting guides and other weighty residents falling into soakaways. This invariably destroys the system beyond repair so your camp hand starts a new hole next to the old one. Again. Like poor old Sisyphus with his endless bouldering, the task that never ends. All maintenance staff fear the need to inspect, let alone repair, the septic tank systems for a very good reason: they are full of other people's shit. So, if I were to suggest that the safari life is an endless sunset, casting warm hues over the remains of yet another rewarding day, I would be lying. If you don't believe me, read on.

I have already introduced the magical floating world of the Kubu Queen houseboat. One of the initial attractions to a young camp manager was the naive assumption that the life aquatic would somehow separate me from the more mundane aspects of camp maintenance. That included the very many plumbing catastrophes for which remote camps are known. I was literally sailing away from all of that terrestrial trauma, clear skies above and fresh waters below.

An obvious design flaw of the Kubu Queen was the addition of a small on-board bathroom that contained a serviceable toilet. Once you offer paying customers a facility like this, trust me, they tend to use it. This only served to exacerbate the more profound design flaw to be found lurking beneath the polished teak decking. The houseboat had a vast fuel tank, possibly a castoff from a retired navy destroyer, that almost filled the hull. The small pocket of remaining gloom below deck housed a septic tank borrowed from a large doll's house. Had I been able to access the void, I would have switched the inlet pipes around for a much more suitable arrangement. The original owner had apparently just moored up alongside a riverside lodge and pumped the boat's diminutive bowels dry. Simple.

Lacking a permanent mooring, my own schedule was relaxed. Essentially a world without end, limited only by charter flight timetables and my own enthusiasm for seeking out trouble in the furthest navigable corners of the Okavango Delta. I might have four days allocated to steam through the heart of darkness, which was wonderful, except my septic tank had a two-day range at best. It would be exceptionally bad form to pump raw sewage into the reed filtered river and, both environmentally and morally, I was quite opposed to that idea. I was clear where I stood regarding this faecal matter, but I was far less clear on what I was actually going to do about it on a practical level. I couldn't access base camp, as this was too far from my primary area of operations for the slow-moving houseboat, so perhaps the camp could reach me? An idea that seemed quite sound in the confines of the Jedibe Island Camp bar started to feel progressively unsound once I was two days upriver.

Halfway through a bottle of malbec, I decided that a speed boat containing two empty fuel drums would be a fair alternative to a soakaway. That was four hundred litres of empty space into which I could pump the foul contents from below deck. The only other piece of kit required was a petrol pump capable of handling effluent, known in the trade as a *honey sucker*. The speed boat could tie alongside the houseboat with the pump's output pipe stuck in the two hundred litre drum, it sounded simple enough. I figured that, if we were careful, I would be ready for the next group of clients needing the 'head' within the hour.

Despite a nagging doubt, toxic transfer day arrived. I moored in a wide lagoon four hours from camp and waited for the sewage cavalry to arrive. In the early morning calm, watching my hand-tied fly drift amongst some lily pads, I wondered if the cautious bream had any idea what we were about to attempt. I hadn't even attracted a nibble before I heard the drone of an outboard across the papyrus. The camp's oldest speed boat swung into the lagoon with no less than four staff lounging in the dented aluminium hull. It was clear that this was considered an easy duty, better than a day raking pathways or painting reed fence panels with creosote. The man at the tiller, a dapper young Motswana called Julius, pulled alongside and deftly tied off his stern painter to a spare cleat.

'Morning Julius!' I called and nodded to his crew, 'morning chaps!'

Smiles all round, some jokes and a slow organisation of gear and men. We had been through a theoretical training session on dry land. That had been tolerated with bored good humour, really, how hard could it be? I climbed up to the top deck where I could see exactly what was going on and offered a few obvious pointers such as ensuring the pipes were being connected properly and that the pump was being primed. It was so simple that two of the crew were chatting and smoking in the bow, happy observers. I had one final warning, 'When you start the pump, run it at low throttle because that barrel is going to fill fast!'

Shambolic

Julius waved my concerns away and his lieutenant grinned and pointed the outlet hose confidently into the barrel.

I wondered if this was the strange calm that always precedes the storm. That thought was cut short by the sudden throb of the pump spinning to life as Julius gave the starter rope a hefty pull. A haze of oily blue smoke drifted across the lagoon and the air filled with the harsh clatter of the over-stressed petrol engine. Julius had decided to keep the throttle wide open despite my considered opinion and the guy holding the business end of the pipe looked startled by the pressure being generated.

'Not so fast!' I shouted into the din of the motor and the gushing of whatever the hell it was shooting down the pipe. The only person in the boat that was no longer looking worried was Julius, still happily racing his honey sucker at full bore. The pipeman was trying to peer into the narrow opening and began shouting something to Julius; he looked tense. Julius shouted something back and nobody did anything to alter their fate. As surely as if Julius were leading his doomed dragoons into Tennyson's valley of death, nothing would ever be the same again. What happened next still haunts the dreams of those involved.

The fuel drum suddenly flexed which signified its fullness. The pump kept running at race pace. Then came the inevitable and terrible explosion as the sewage ran out of tank space and sought a new home. The first gusher was about ten metres high and started a rain of very localised filth onto the occupants of the small boat. Initially I threw myself behind the cover of the bar. Realising that both the interior of the houseboat and I seemed to be untouched by this monstrous storm, I slowly raised my head above the parapet.

Peering over the side of the houseboat I noted that the catastrophe was largely confined to the tender boat. One of the crew had thrown himself into the lagoon and was attempting to swim beyond fallout range, fear of crocodiles forgotten in the face of an immediate and superior terror. His smoking companion had jumped onto the stern of the houseboat and seemed to be faring quite well in a protected corner. The situation inside the tender, though, was dire.

It was as though I was looking through a window into the guts of hell itself. The pipeman was incredibly still, holding the pipe and screaming incoherently whilst he drowned in shit. This was like a scene in the movies where they strike oil, except this wasn't black gold. Julius was holding both hands over his head in a futile act of self-preservation as he sat in half a metre (and rising) of effluent. Only when the level reached the full metre mark did he reach up and switch the pump off. The trauma of being showered in the unspeakable had apparently paralysed his central nervous system. Happily, the Kubu Queen and her skipper were still spotless, but I can say that I am one of the few humans alive to have seen a small boat and two men painted in crap.

Once the shower ceased, the horror of the situation relaxed its numbing grip on both men and they hurled themselves into the water to furiously scrub away their shame. Their companions were howling with laughter, the best medicine apparently, although it didn't appear to be reviving the spirits of Julius and his lieutenant much. Julius was draped in lily pad stems and river weed, spluttering and cursing. The turd of the Kraken sprang to mind. There was no way to clean the tender so the cursed crew motored from the lagoon with most of the houseboat's waste and every fly in northern Botswana onboard. Their clothes were draped over the sides and their feet were braced well above the slopping deck. It would take a press gang to find anyone willing to attempt a repeat performance.

I hauled anchor and put as much distance between myself and the scene of the crime as possible.

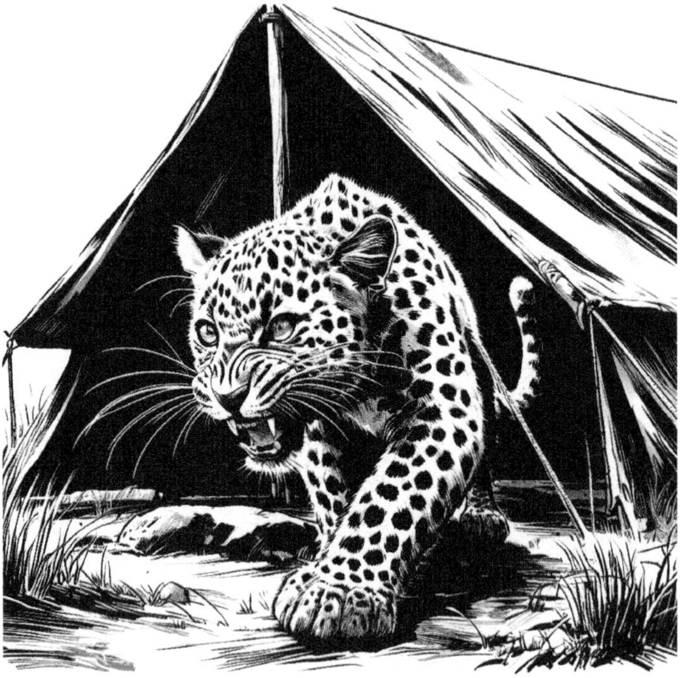

Savuti

In 1998, the company offered me my own piece of real estate to manage in the Savuti Channel. I knew the area well because it was on the same private concession as Dumatau. The previous manager had gone loco, convinced that the local lion pride were out to get him. In a drunken rage of paranoia, he had taken a potshot at one of his maned tormentors. Unfortunately, he had chosen to go on the offensive from the camp bar, which contained a couple of startled guests sipping cocktails. By the time he was cooling his heals in a Jo'burg funny farm, I was on a small plane out of the Delta reading a metre long fax entitled, 'How to run Savuti Bush Camp.' Typically, incoming managers get a few weeks of handover with the outgoing boss. I was getting the budget version, just a list of staff, key operational duties and some comedian at head office had drawn a lion waving six-shooters on the bottom of the fax.

It would be fair to say that the camp staff were a little dysfunctional, probably because their previous manager had more ticks than an old jackal. The most important front-of-house staff in any camp are the managers, the guides and the barman, not necessarily in that order. At Savuti I found a depressed polit-agitator for a barman, a rebel without a specific cause. If ever a human had fallen into the wrong profession, it was my emotionally downcast bar steward. Freud would have filled notebooks with observations.

On my third afternoon I was informed that Simon the barman was

Shambolic

quite literally refusing to rise to the occasion. He was sitting on the floor behind the high-topped bar, apparently on strike. This sort of human resources issue fell squarely on my shoulders. I was mindful of putting down the heavy wrench I had been using to bust loose some rusted bolts before heading to the solo protest.

'What ails thee, Simon?'

This enquiry was met with silence from beneath the polished mahogany countertop. Peering over I could see the top of a head, lowered in mute protest. A long sigh rose from the shady spot, from deep within Simon's tortured person.

'Why must I stand all day, my legs ache, it is hot…'

The sentence trailed off, crushed by existential grief. It reminded me of a line from one of those French art-house films that have neither plot nor purpose. There were six sturdy bar stools within reach of this weary mixologist, so near and yet apparently out of his grasp. Simon was enacting some worker versus the corporate machine role play, with a cast of one. Some gentle truths were called for.

'Chap, you need to stand behind the bar all day because you are the barman. You need to make sure the beers are cold and the wine isn't corked and that your customers don't fall off the deck into the long grass. That's your currently paid job, unless you want some hard work instead?'

Simon was apparently confusing our remote outpost with a democracy, but he was quite wrong, we couldn't afford that degree of civilisation.

'Hard work?' The head cocked to one side.

'Maintenance? Prep in the kitchen?'

Some muffled noise, a shuffling sound and a gradual return to an upright position. Simon was belligerent, certainly melancholy, but he wasn't stupid. The barman in a safari camp is a prime position, light on heavy lifting. A hand slowly rubbed across the bar top with a rag, removing a coffee cup stain. Then a symbolic compromise.

'Maybe I can rest on a chair for some of the day.'

'Maybe you can.'

I walked away from the bar, seriously considering the merits of vending machines versus humans.

Then there was the long-term assistant manager, Tutelife. Experienced, charismatic and a dedicated alcoholic. He was such amiable company though that I granted him a general pass on the boozing. Most of the time he managed to be a functioning alcoholic which sufficed and, quite honestly, was something of a norm in the safari business at the time. On the evenings when he was truly tanked and pissing gin, his girlfriend kept him under house arrest in the staff village. Only once did I have to wrestle him out of a Land Rover when he decided he fancied a midnight game drive after enjoying a few bottles of the house red.

That just left my second guide, the unusually named Arafat. He had grown up near the Chobe National Park which is famous across Africa for the huge concentrations of elephant that converge on the river during the dry season. It was interesting then to learn that Arafat was utterly terrified of elephants. That is a tricky phobia to manage in an area not only filled with the trunk waving hooligans but in a job that encourages as much contact with them as possible. After all, tourists don't fly to Africa to not see elephants.

I became aware of this natural aversion when I was out checking on the local waterholes early in my camp residency. There were a series of water pumps along the dry Savuti Channel that we used to supply fresh water as essential bait for thirsty wildlife. Pachyderms were some of the most enthusiastic supporters of this water welfare programme. I had just refilled the fuel tank on one of the pumps, cranked the handle and stood back as the fly wheels began to spin and deliver water to the waterhole a hundred metres away. All I had to do then was sit on my bull bar and marvel as the nearest herd of elephants thundered out of the bushes to reach the cool, clear liquid.

I knew Arafat was driving with clients somewhere in the neighbourhood and I wanted his punters to experience the sighting. It is standard practice for guides to share interesting sightings.

'Arafat, come in for Ben.'

The pump thumped away like a mechanical heart in the background and I waited for a reply on the radio.

'Ah, Ben, come in.'

Time to share the good news.

'Arafat, I'm at Country Pan with a nice herd of eles.'

Shambolic

All the waterholes had a name; Country Pan, Camp Pan and so on. I had tried to rename one of them Bedpan but it didn't stick for some reason.

'Say again, Ben.'

'There is a big herd of eles at Country Pan. Just started to drink, they'll be here for a while, over.'

'Ah, I'm very far from you, over.'

Which is fair enough, except he wasn't far away because, as we spoke, I saw the dust rising from his vehicle further down the channel.

'Uh, I think I see you Arafat? I'm at Country Pan, over.'

'Ah... Ben.'

Silence and perhaps some questions from his own guests who would also be listening to our conversation.

'I've got a good sighting here, Ben... ground hornbills, over.'

Now, call me old fashioned but if I were paying the price of a decent family car to see the sights of wild Africa, I'd rather be served elephant than bird. Ground hornbills are interesting but only in the way a hot-dog is interesting whilst you wait for the game to start. I had shared the local intel, done my duty and I wasn't about to engage in a debate over value for money on an open radio channel. Arafat's Land Rover disappeared down the channel and, eventually, out of sight. Then I sat back and watched my elephants, a feast of nature for one.

That evening, with our punters happily watching the bush TV, I cornered Arafat in the bar.

'What happened today? You were only ten minutes from those elephants, it was a nice sighting.'

The professional guide started to form a reply and then stopped himself, shoulders sagging in defeat.

'I don't like elephants.'

It wasn't the answer I was expecting. Maybe I should mention that we had walked together into lions around camp on several occasions and Arafat had been as cool as a cucumber. Pachyderm-ophobia, I would never have guessed.

'You don't like elephants? Why not?'

'They want to kill me.'

He said it with utter conviction, without drama, as though it were the eleventh commandment. I knew he had been guiding at the camp for over two years already, clearly developing some elaborate game of dodge the ele. I hadn't had a single punter complain, so live and let live seemed like a way forwards for the both of us.

'Alright, my friend, stick to the cats and dogs.'

Luckily, Savuti had more than enough predators to thrill our guests.

You might think this sounds like a motley crew of fools but safari camps are just small communities, populated by the same neuroses that perpetuate in the real world. Nobody seems to notice because safaris dazzle. That and the fact that the camp and surrounding area delivered action on a level almost beyond imagining.

The Savuti Channel once linked the great Selinda Spillway with the Okavango Delta but shifting tectonic plates beneath the sand had stopped the flow of water. It left behind a dry riverbed which became the focal point for some of Africa's most documented predator turf wars. The backdrop for a long running feud between clans of hyenas and, at the time, Botswana's biggest lion pride led by the feline don King Savuti. The Savuti pride was so numerous and so perpetually hungry that it shifted from hunting antelope and zebra to elephants. Guides and guests had front row seats for some unbelievable scenes with big cats hanging off the haunches of huge pachyderms and slowly dragging them to the ground. The elephant herd might rally and try to chase the lions away and rescue their stricken comrade. Typically, the rescue would be short lived as the bleeding and shocked elephant would prove too tempting for this mega-pride of lions to walk away from. It could be somewhat distressing; humans are fundamentally biased towards the good guy and what kind of sick individual murders the good guy in the baggy pants? So, humans and elephants alike were often left traumatized by the violent antics of King Savuti's cat cult.

I took over Savuti Bush Camp in the epilogue of King Savuti's reign. The old king was toppled by his three eldest sons. He gave them life, protected them throughout their privileged lives and they repaid him in the style of all ungrateful offspring. They killed their aging father in a short, vicious battle before splitting the pride into three groups. Their short-term gain was overshadowed by their long-term loss because they hadn't grasped the point behind their father's unification strategy. Strong leaders build monopolies for a simple reason; they stop pointless infighting and allow you to dominate all your numerically weaker enemies. The princes put themselves at a severe disadvantage in the numbers game. Savuti's hyenas, those bad guys of the bedtime story scene, watched all of this, cackling from the shadows. They weren't grieving the passing of the king; they saw an opportunity. One unstoppable feline force had been divided into three lesser prides. The era of lion dominance in the Savuti Channel was at an end. Hyena confidence was sky high and they began to harass the lions at any opportunity. Chasing them off kills, stealing their food, trying to kill cubs and mobbing prides just for the hell of it. Epic doesn't come close.

Savuti was an unfenced camp, so it usually wasn't necessary to go looking for wildlife, it frequently came to us. You might wonder what attracts wild animals into a camp full of humans and their human noise? For their part, the elephants were obsessed with those water holes I kept pumped along the channel. If I let them run dry, the elephants just came into camp and pushed over my two 5,000 litre water towers and ripped up the water pipes around camp. I only made that mistake once or maybe twice.

The lions too would come into camp looking for shade, food and sometimes just to freak everyone out. Many mornings began with a warning call from tent to tent, 'Lions in camp, stay in bed, late start this morning!'

Nothing to do but go back to bed and wait for them to move off. Once, after a very, very late night at the campfire, I admit I used the lion excuse as a chance for another hour in bed, the guests were far too scared to ever check outside. The lions made their presence felt by lazing across pathways and sometimes dozing on the decks of tents. Like furry furniture, with teeth.

We had a young male leopard who made the camp his home for two months, he was a bit more of a challenge. I first found him sleeping underneath a solar panel behind my tent. A week later, the evening tranquillity was split by a petrified shriek, an old woman perhaps or a teenage girl? No, a thirty-year-old bush pilot who was joined in his shower by our young leopard. The camp builder had designed a nice outside bathroom around the base of an acacia tree and our whiskered stalker had ambled along the lowest branch just above the preening pilot. I don't know who got the biggest shock, but it worried me that the cat had so little respect for boundaries around humans.

Three days later I was lying on my bed reading and glimpsed movement by my foot. Moving my book aside, I saw a dazzling pair of golden-amber eyes and some very fine whiskers edging through the open flaps of my tent. Not good I thought, not a good thing to be trapped in a tent with a killing machine. I had no plan of action beyond keeping both of us calm. I moved my book slightly to make sure he knew I was awake and aware. That stopped his progress and he was now almost half his body length into my tent and watching me with an unreadable expression. He had clearly thought the tent was empty when he first arrived and now he had a decision to make.

His tail was hanging, which I took as a good sign, flicking tails usually mean it is playtime and I was the closest chew toy. Despite a pounding pulse, it was quite a moment and I wondered if this was the last time my internal organs were going to be just that, internal. After what was probably just seconds but felt like an age, the curious cat reversed slowly back onto the deck and stood watching me through the mozzie mesh. I stayed where I was and took a gulp of air as the leopard turned to casually trot back into the long grass of the channel. It was good to be in one piece and not have my guts decorating the inside of the tent like some horrific bunting. I spent the next five minutes just staring at the slight gap in the grass that he had left but he didn't return.

That close shave led to some discussion with the wildlife authorities who felt he might need to be shot as a dangerous animal. I cut communications off after that, determined to handle our resident cat and keep him safe from over-zealous officials. Sadly, he stopped coming to visit and none of the guides would see him on their game drives again. I think he met a bigger territorial male who would have killed him or chased him away. I like to think he survived and moved to a better home.

Cats might have been a crowd pleaser at Savuti Bush Camp but, for me, it was the wild dogs who really brought the magic. Their approach was typically heralded by an audible warning, a rustle as they bounced down the channel, hopping into the air to look for prey and each other. Imagine a pack of Tiggers, a very wonderful thing, and you won't be far off.

They had a routine that involved chasing an impala into camp and trapping it in the pathway system, using the wooden railings and tents as their ambush points. Our response was just to stop what we were doing and watch the mayhem unfold. It happened so often that Matengu, the surly camp hand, would continue trimming back bushes as the dog pack swirled around him in a flurry of yelps and tails.

One morning the entire pack caught a young impala on the deck of the honeymoon tent and, in my enthusiasm to share the moment, I rounded up all the guests and took them down to watch the grisly show. We sat and watched the slaughter for a few minutes before I noticed a face peering anxiously back at us through the shade cloth window of the tent. It seemed the young honeymooners were still at home, still in bed, doing honeymoon stuff and weren't thrilled to be part of the morning game viewing. I gathered my camera-snapping mob together and left them in relative peace, although the murder of an antelope three feet from your bed isn't likely to do much for the libido. When they arrived for brunch, we all kept our heads down and pretended we hadn't spent the morning gawping at them in bed as the backdrop to the wild dog hunt.

These natural distractions were like mainlining serotonin to an admin dodger like me. On occasion though, the admin just wouldn't be denied my full attention.

One cool winter morning I was woken by a gently spoken, 'Knock! Knock!'

Spoken, because you can't knock on a canvas tent, not if you want anyone to notice anyway.

'Ben... are you awake?'

It was my sidekick, Tutelife.

'Tuts? Everything OK?'

I replied from under a pile of comforting blankets, trying to remember if I had forgotten to rise early for some task or other.

'The staff village bathroom is *stukkend!*'

He used the Afrikaans word for broken.

It was still dark. Only a few early shift staff would be up and about but, in a few hours, the wash block would be getting some heavy traffic. I pulled on my chinos and a military parka to stumble out into what would become another memorable day for all involved. We walked silently together through the bush in a direct shortcut to the staff village, torches swinging in the endless hunt for big cats who were a constant presence around camp. Tuts was armed with a wooden walking staff and I had a six-cell maglite; we could handle almost anything apart from the hideous foe towards which we were walking.

The staff village was predictably quiet with a couple of faint lights showing through windows here and there. The communal wash block was devoid of customers and when the smell hit us, I understood why. The stench was eye watering. I flushed a toilet to see what would happen and immediately heard a bizarre bubbling sound, like a geo-thermal mud pot. Investigating at the back of the building we discovered Botswana's largest man-made lake. I was fairly sure it hadn't been there when I was last in the staff village a few days prior.

'This is bad, Tuts.'

'Maybe Matengu knows how to fix it?'

Tuts invoked the name of our surly camp hand and head of the maintenance team. I say 'head', but in truth he was the only member of the maintenance team. I had witnessed Matengu attempt all manner of repair shortcuts, frequently rendering the equipment he was attempting to repair completely useless. He had only recently been banned from using power tools without express permission. A long screw had been sticking out of a teak floorboard, a job for our single precious screw gun. The posi-drive bit had dropped out and fallen under the decking. Matengu's solution was to simply turn the power tool around and use the handle as a hammer to smash the screw back through the floor. He had also smashed the handle into sharp plastic shards; we went back to old fashioned screwdrivers after that. The only reason he still worked at the camp was because his wife was an excellent housekeeper. I couldn't face losing her talents and so I chose to overlook his deficits. As it turned

Shambolic

out, Matengu had literally got wind of the plumbing problem and was keeping himself busy at the opposite end of camp on some mysterious maintenance project.

It was late morning before I had assembled enough crew to tackle the job. It should have been early in the morning, but it had taken hours to corner enough volunteers. The most junior staff had concealed themselves in various ingenious locations as soon as word spread that we had a major sewage issue to resolve. Our artillery consisted of a heavy-duty water pump with fifteen metres of bright yellow fire hose. Matengu *had* to be there, Tuts was keeping our guests happy and I had collared two of the trackers as unwilling support. Our chef had wandered over to see what was going on and insisted that he would be a great help. I was divided over the need to keep him nice and clean for his primary role in the kitchen and being impressed by his enthusiasm. When I suggested he stay out of this particular drama he looked so crestfallen that I relented and, as it happened, he became quite the star player in our comedy of errors.

Our initial problem was simply locating the submerged septic tank. Something was clearly blocking it, be it a warthog, a pair of trousers or something larger that had been flushed into the system. To discover the cause we first had to put the wide septic lake somewhere else. By great good fortune there was an unused pit twelve metres away, the soakaway for a second septic tank that had not been installed. Whilst unfinished, size-wise it was enough for our needs.

I pulled rank and designated the task of pump operation to my unhappy maintenance chief. He accepted this burden of seniority with barely concealed disgust. It had to be him really, the two trackers were hiding behind a Jackalberry tree at that point. We dragged the petrol pump to a midway point with one pipe trailing away into the earthy void. The inlet pipe was tossed as far into the foetid swamp as Matengu could manage without the risk of getting splashed. He double checked every connection and any port from which sewage might escape. I considered a worst-case scenario and retreated to a distance that would be beyond any fallout. Generally, I believe that you need to lead from the front in every situation, except ones like this when remote control is adequate.

Eventually, Matengu was satisfied. He took one last baleful look at me and hauled on the starter rope. The engine caught, the signature oily blue exhaust drifted into the trees and the sound of gushing fluid resonated from the pit. He stood up, visibly relaxing and shrugged whilst his two assistants ventured out from behind their cover.

Chef was looking into the slowly filling pit and cracking jokes.

'Eh monnas! Too much big barbel fish in here,' he shouted, 'someone fetch my fishing pole!'

The sense of doom that had hung over the operation was lifting. In a slightly surprising turn of events, the plan appeared to be working. It was clear that the pumping would take a while before we could see anything of use in the flooded area and everyone started to find other ways to entertain themselves. Carlos the tracker fetched his guitar to liven the gathering up. He had made it himself from a Castrol GTX can, a broomstick for a neck and two strings made from heavy fishing line. He strummed while Chef started singing about the fish he was going to cook for supper. I wasn't hungry. The music was briefly interrupted by a pride of lions who sauntered through the mopane trees a few hundred metres away. Nobody was worried, they wouldn't come anywhere near the slowly receding inland lake. They ambled back into thicker bush. Someone flushed a toilet in the wash block. Matengu wasn't amused at this counterproductive action and shouted some mild abuse at the startled staff member who scuttled up the path into the village.

I had a number of things that I should be doing besides counting other people's turds and decided Matengu and Carlos could handle operations until the septic tank emerged from the mire. No sooner had I turned away when the fire hose went slack and the flow of effluent stopped abruptly. The pump continued to run but to no effect. There was clearly still pressure in the pipe running from the wash block reservoir, so there had to be a blockage inside the pump itself.

Considering my past experiences of shit hitting the fan, this was not a welcome development. The only safe way to proceed was to turn the pump off, open the housing and find the blockage. A reasonably low risk process which I intended to outsource to the camp handyman.

Before I could suggest any of this, Chef walked over to the pump and bent down to get a closer look. I assumed he was reaching for the off-switch but instead he started twisting the screw cap that opens the pump's intake chamber. This is only used to prime the pump with fresh water and never when it is running, it is a simple fluid under pressure scenario.

I started to shout a warning as Chef managed to unscrew the cap completely. So began the second fountain of filth to which I have been an unwilling witness. The pump did an excellent impression of that scene from *The Exorcist,* the epic demonic barf that the possessed seem to enjoy directing at the clergy.

Sadly, I knew how this scene was going to play out as the immediate area around the pump was being showered in bilge. Carlos had fled but his guitar was getting soaked. There wouldn't be any music for a while. Matengu actually ran *through* a wheelbarrow, so rapid and focussed was his desire to escape. There was a reverberating bang as he hit the solid metal and then he just carried straight on through, a molecular miracle powered by fear. This feat was better than David Copperfield at the Great Wall of China. Our junior tracker, who had only recently emerged from behind his tree, turned and ran straight into the half-full pit. There was no excuse for that sort of stupidity, even in dire circumstances. He floundered there for a couple of shocked seconds before managing to haul himself out using the firehose. He then ran screaming to the staff village where he would need hosing down and probably some trauma therapy to resolve his post traumatic stress disorder.

Meanwhile, Chef, who clearly felt responsible for this mess, was preparing for a second attack on the faulty pump. He had found an ancient Marigold pink rubber glove and was using it as protection for his right hand. The logic of this evaded me as the rest of him was going to be doused the second he was in range of the spewing machine. I had chosen a termite mound as my command post, well beyond the putrid precipitation, and could do little more than marvel at Chef's foolhardy charge. A one-man forlorn hope. Again, I assumed the off switch was his target but again I was wrong.

Ignoring the obvious solution to his problem, he began frantically searching for the cap that had been blasted off the pump. Brave, reckless and apparently happy to prolong his suffering in a fundamentally pointless task. Incredibly, he discovered the small cap in a spreading puddle of horror and screwed it back into place. This immediately brought the unhealthy shower to a stop and the pump began to deliver the sewage to our chosen destination once more. Chef had fixed what he had broken, not that I was going to shake his rubber clad hand over his success. I offered a thumbs-up and excused him from further latrine duties.

As he walked dripping back towards the village, he met a scullery girl who shrieked at the hideous apparition before her and fled back the way she had come. Chef could have walked unmolested through the worst ghetto on the continent, he was literally untouchable. Matengu had returned to complete physical form and was looking very pleased with himself. He had remained as clean as the head of maintenance was ever going to get. Carlos was gazing unhappily at his ruined instrument,

'Shit...' he muttered to himself.

It was now low tide in the devil's pool and the septic tank had emerged like a wreck from the deep. Matengu was looking into the open mouth of the plastic tank with a level of curiosity I hadn't seen in him before. He fetched a length of *lata* pole and returned to begin prodding something concealed inside the great container. After a brief fishing expedition, the pole was lifted clear with what was once a white running takkie attached to the end. Matengu swung his discovery towards me for inspection. It wasn't obvious if the owner of the shoe was still in the tank. The only other way it could have ended up in there was if someone had eaten it first. Either way, it appeared that we had resolved the problem and Matengu took the shoe and headed back to the staff village. I hoped he wasn't planning to take up one-legged athletic training.

We had all survived the unwelcome brush with our misfiring plumbing and the only place I wanted to be was in the bar with my unionised bar keeper.

'Sorry about your guitar, Carlos,' I offered my despondent tracker consolation.

'Shit...' he muttered to himself.

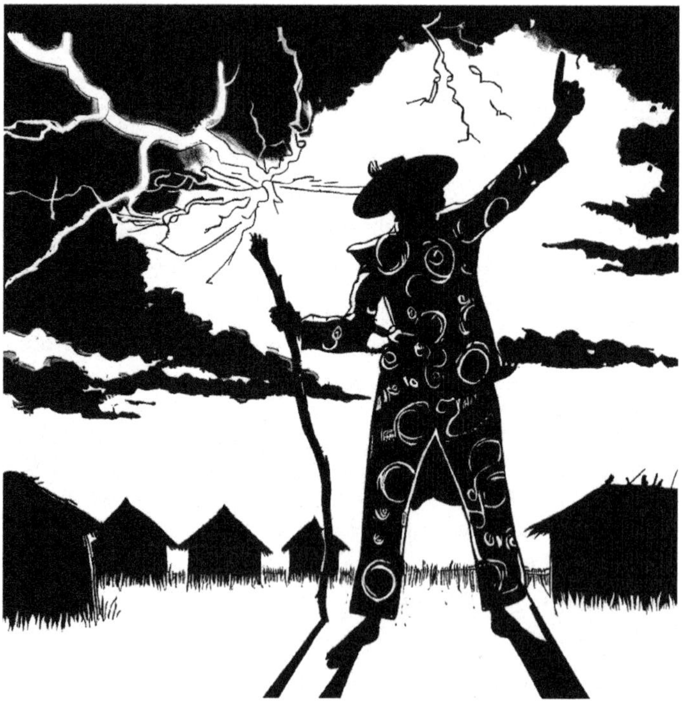

The Witch Doctor

It was an oppressively hot day, a dog day, with an unfiltered sun pulsing through the air around me. I was sitting in a wheelbarrow which itself was radiating a painful heat. The prevailing swelter enveloped me in an energy sapping shroud. A lit cigarette dangled between my limp fingers became something of a focal point, pointless but fascinating. There were children and goats being noisy somewhere nearby whilst a figure detached itself from the last row of huts in the village. The super-heated air gave the figure the appearance of elevating, moving closer without a connection to the earth beneath us. That made sense, more sense than the cigarette at least which still smouldered like an extra digit.

Then the figure was right in front of me, holding out a chipped enamel mug. This startled me into a bolt upright position and I took the mug instinctively, rude not to accept a gift? Later, I was alone again in the wheelbarrow, staring at the cigarette and the small flowers that decorated the rim of the mug. Suddenly both objects evoked a wave of choking nausea as the relentless sun beat me further into numb submission.

As a brilliant diversion, a small aircraft landed pretty much right in front of me, covering both me and the mug in a fine layer of dust. This was a huge relief, something completely familiar, something relevant to my life. I was vaguely aware that someone had climbed out of the

Shambolic

aircraft and was demanding to know why an idiot in a wheelbarrow was sitting on the airstrip. It was an excellent question and I wanted to know the answer as well, time to clear this mess up. That enquiry died mid-air when my girlfriend arrived to pull me out of the wheelbarrow and steer me, like the village drunk, towards the pilot.

'Don't worry,' she explained, 'he's got malaria.'

That changed the negative atmosphere. The pilot draped my slack arm over his shoulder and they hauled me to the aircraft. I spilt the water over him and lost the cigarette in the dust. The mug went with me into the back of the cramped cabin where I passed out amongst a pile of worn canvas mail bags. Essential equipment requests, stock take results, love letters, golfing magazines and an unconscious human.

Two days later I was semi-coherent, in Maun, the wonders of modern medicine having purged my system of the worst of my fever-state. The repetitive nausea and the delirium dreams had retreated to be replaced by a dull ache in my limbs and the energy levels typically associated with the very elderly.

Despite the unpromising start to the month, there was a silver lining of sorts. It was the start of my leave cycle which meant I had a full four weeks to forget about the whole miserable malaria experience. We planned to get out of Botswana as fast as possible, fly to Johannesburg and pick the most exotic sounding destination on the international departures board. To that end, we had booked our flights south, I had a stash of chemical *pick me ups* for use in a pinch and, crucially, four months' pay and tips. The universe took a long cold look at me and decided that malaria wasn't a true test of a human, there were other ways to challenge youthful *joie de vivre*.

On day two in town, I woke with nothing better to do than take a long cool shower and watch the kingfishers darting beyond the chain mesh fence of the company plot. Silvia had gone into town on some last-minute shopping mission. Maybe a late breakfast at one of the lodges that dotted the riverbank before catching our afternoon flight?

As I relaxed under the brackish Maun water, someone else came to a personal crossroads in their life. A random decision, an endless series of which is surely the fabric of life? My unlocked door was their first decision of the day: in or out? Then, clearly committed, this master criminal made off with my entire cash reserve that I had carefully hidden in plain sight on top of my bed.

As soon as I walked into the spartan room, dripping fresh from my shower, I knew something was wrong. My wallet, which was a canvas airline ticket folder, had lost its healthy swell. Like a prize dairy cow suddenly shrivelled by rinderpest, its former potential evaporated in a moment. The folder still sat on top of the bed but it had moved a few feet and had that unmistakably discarded look about it. My brain still wasn't firing on all cylinders as I picked it up and stared into its emptiness. Imagine a drunk being tricked by a children's entertainer. I stared hard, turned the folder over, looked from every angle and then resumed pointless contemplation of the empty interior. It was definitely empty apart from a weird fifty Krona note someone had tipped me. The thief had actually rejected that single bank note, which only made it more personal.

To be robbed is traumatic enough, but to be selectively robbed is tragic. It had been a long four months in the bush, with some tricky clients, a number of staff problems ranging from near-mutiny in the bar, to a staff member nearly bleeding to death as I assembled a DIY rescue package for her. I had earned that cash, a bulging stack of Rand, US dollars, British pounds, even some greasy over-used paper currency from Zimbabwe courtesy of a thankful professional guide who was proud enough to honour the ancient custom of baksheesh despite being broke. In the safari world, monthly wages are obviously essential but tips are the legacy earned through sweat and occasional virtuosity that matter. One is for living, the other for living out dreams, or at least buying more air mileage.

Powerful chemicals and malarial fatigue were just adding to the depressing fog of anti-climax. My legs aching, I walked back to the door. Propped up by the worn frame, I scanned the courtyard for signs. Any mischievous head poking around the corner? A friend with a sick sense of humour (I had plenty) or a really amateur thief determined to gloat over their great good fortune a little longer in near proximity? There was nothing to see, just dusty footprints, peeling paint, corrugated tin roofing, blue sky, nothing that was going to help me. I looked back to the wallet in my increasingly sweaty hands and stared into the void that still held the vague shape of a wedge of bank notes.

Then, frantically, in a panic, I took the room to pieces, emptying bags onto the floor, pulling drawers out of their runners, dragging a wardrobe away from the wall. I found a dead rat, checked under the dead rat and flipped the bed. It was completely pointless because I had left the money on the bed and now it was gone. It was time to share my grief, so I pulled on a pair of shorts and went looking for an emotional support human.

Considering that the company plot was a last resort for tired staff visiting from the remote camps and hungover overland guides resting between safaris, the emotional support was limited. In life, you are often alone in your personal triumphs and it is the same in grief. The very laws of natural selection depend on extended periods of good fortune. Genetics matter but so does knowing when to duck. I was reminded of this instantly as I watched a small number of my friends and colleagues offer their condolences before rushing off to check the whereabouts of their own valuables. Once it was clear that I was the fated lottery loser for the day, people mostly wanted to hear how much money had gone. Bad luck is curiously entertaining to those it has yet to touch. I wasn't entertained though, I was trying to calculate the odds of reversing this twist of fate.

The company plot was located far from town, on the riverside with villages and private homes scattered around. The security system consisted of a high chain mesh fence and locked gates. In reality this wasn't so much for the benefit of the transient staff population but rather to protect the company fleet and workshops. The thief had simply run into a lucky moment of careless money management in a generally cash-poor environment. My only glimmer of light was that the thief technically worked or was staying at the plot. I didn't need Poirot to explain that, as the crime had happened less than thirty minutes previously, that same person was probably still on site. The money was probably hidden somewhere in the sprawling compound, my precious, just beyond my fevered fingertips.

It was time to get the law involved. A friend had a contact in Maun

CID and promised to get some professional help whilst I started rounding up the occupants of the plot. It seemed like an obvious first step, gather potential witnesses, discount the majority and hopefully squeeze a culprit out of the group. A couple of friends offered to handle some pre-police interrogation and there was one offer of straight up violence for the cause. I thought the law might take a dim view if they were to arrive and discover us holding a skinny mechanic's assistant upside down whilst we beat the soles of his feet with ostrich feathers. No, I was confident a detective from CID would be able to sort this out, I don't know why I thought that and later I wished we had gone straight for option A.

The police arrived in a Toyota double cab with a light bar on the roof, so far so good. The detective had a regular cop in tow, clearly on a look and learn assignment. His superior was straight out of the *Starsky and Hutch* wardrobe department; he had a tired looking brown suit, a grubby collar and brown plastic shoes. He was a fairly unusual shape as well, about one and a half metres tall and a metre wide at the middle. I had never seen such a short policeman, slightly dwarfed by his lanky uniformed minion. My friend, who had called his local police contact for help, shook his head in bemused impotence.

As I stepped forward to introduce myself, the detective turned away and barked out a few commands in Tswana. His sidekick shuffled the gathered staff and visitors into an untidy line. The rogue's gallery consisted of nine permanent staff – mechanics, laundry girls and gardeners. Then six staff visiting from various camps, guides, a couple of managers and one overland guide who lived at the plot between safaris. The two groups were separated, one on parade and the other more of a peanut gallery of curious bystanders.

The detective turned and sized me up with a piercing stare that bordered on unhinged. It wasn't clear what his intentions were. In the meantime, the other cop decided to arrange the line of suspects in height order. This generated some muffled laughter which he ignored until he had everything in perfect order. I suspect he would have been a good flower arranger.

'Now, who do you suspect?' said the CID man loudly, expectantly and directly to me. Everyone stared as if I were about to reveal some great mystery, the final scene in the play. Kicking the can down the road a little way is one thing but this seemed like a complete role reversal. Traditionally, I always thought this was the policeman's job, the crime solving part, that is.

'Well,' you could hear a pin drop by this point, 'I don't know *who* exactly because I didn't witness the theft, it just seems likely that it was someone who works here, because they would have had access to my room.'

It seemed diplomatic enough considering we were discussing a group of people who were all listening from a few feet away.

'If someone had broken into the plot, they would be pretty obvious, a stranger walking about...'

A couple of nods in agreement from the team of mechanics and the uniformed cop. The detective wasn't giving up on that line of enquiry yet.

'Why couldn't it be someone else from the community?'

Surely it had to be easier to start with the small group of candidates at hand rather than begin a random manhunt through northern Botswana? The compound was eight kilometres from town, surrounded by a chain link fence, and a strange face would stick out worse than the detective's apparent lack of competency.

'Well, everyone here was present when the theft took place, it seems like there is a chance that one of them was involved.'

Less diplomatic but I wanted to get Poirot back on track.

'Oh!' replied the detective, losing interest in his theory.

He turned to the waiting line, fixing them with his piercing glare. One of the laundry girls whimpered, the mechanics smirked and a gardener was pushed back into line. I had never been involved in official thief identification but it appeared to be going badly. The CID man began walking along the back of the line, stopping every few paces to stare intensely at his chosen targets, textbook intimidation. The uniformed cop wrote something down in a notebook which attracted his superior's attention. He walked over to peer down at the page, then he walked back to me and asked if I had any further theories on the identity of the thief. I heard a groan of dismay from behind me and knew it was my friend with the police contacts.

'Well, the mechanics work at the far end of the compound from my room, so I doubt they would know anything about it.'

I had also already spoken to their boss, the chief mechanic who lived at the plot and he confirmed everyone had been with him in the grease pit all morning.

'Is this true?' Poirot asked the nearest mechanic.

'Yes,' he replied with the confident tone of a man with a solid alibi, 'we don't see nothing!'

'Well, go back to work then!' The detective delivered it like a threat, as if he knew what was going on here.

The uniform wrote something down in his notebook, probably line minus 4. Whilst all of this drama was slowly unfolding, the two gardeners had been staring forlornly at the dusty ground and one of them was sweating quite profusely despite the cool early morning air. I thought this looked suspicious but I was, apparently, in a minority. The cops were watching the mechanics walk away and nodding with satisfaction. If they couldn't decide who had stolen the money, maybe it was enough to decide who *hadn't* stolen it?

'Perhaps you should search these people?'

I was getting bored standing around and watching the line of suspects sweat. The senior policeman looked genuinely surprised at the suggestion, but he rolled with it and snapped a command to his subordinate. The uniform told everyone to empty out their pockets. One of the laundry girls had a matchbox which he took, slowly turning it in his hands before making a show of shaking the little cardboard oblong close to his right ear. He then slid the box open to reveal… matches.

'Good grief…' muttered someone from the friends and family camp.

The uniform slowly walked down the line inspecting open palms, stopping to admire a small brass button in the shaking hand of one of the gardeners. This shrub wrangler was now the dictionary definition of guilty as sin and I couldn't imagine a better time to put some pressure on him for a full confession. The cop, though, had other ideas and told everyone to remove their shoes. The line wobbled as everyone removed one shoe and balanced on the other foot. One of the older laundry ladies even removed a sock to show her willingness. The footwear was empty of both feet and foreign currency and the cop was finished with that line of enquiry. He had only checked about twenty per cent of the possible hiding places on an adult human, but who would hide a wedge of stolen cash anywhere except their pocket or in their right shoe?

The detective swivelled and pointed towards the small group of my friends who were now lounging along a low wall.

'What about them?'

'I work with those guys,' I reasoned, 'they don't have to rob me, they fleece tourists all year.'

That, and the fact that they were my friends and it seemed more likely that this was a random act of opportunity rather than some oddly personal hate crime. The cop didn't look convinced as he stared the group down.

Clearly a token room search was in order. In the interests of avoiding claims of favouritism it was a sound enough move but it was also a further waste of time. The first room was torn apart to the amusement of Muddy, the overland guide who lived there a few days each month. The uniform discovered a copy of *Hustler* under the mattress and went to work investigating that until the detective took it off him and tucked it under his arm. They then found a jar full of loose change, which the thief-taker general held aloft with a grunt of satisfaction. His expression fell when he held the shrapnel towards me and I shook my head in a silent negative. Muddy reclaimed his cigarette money and the crime-busting duo moved on to the next room. It slowly became obvious this was leading them nowhere and the CID man decided he wanted to search the homes of the compound staff, mostly in the nearest small village. It was impossible that the money would have gone that far. If the thief was still in the company plot, then so was my money, stuffed in some dark corner like a forgotten dream.

Half an hour later, the cops returned from their property search with a size thirteen spanner taken from the workshop and three boxes of soap detergent from the laundry. They seemed extremely pleased with their progress, but I wondered if they had forgotten what they were actually looking for. It wasn't a surprise when the detective announced that he was done for the time being and gave me his card should I have any further questions for him. He turned to the line-up and waved a stubby finger, 'I will be watching you all!'

Then he was gone, back to the office and probably an early start to his weekend. The gardeners stared in amazement, they were free to go, no apparent consequences or questioning from the law.

Life is full of moments when you are apparently powerless to affect a positive outcome on your own. The system that is designed to support you turns out to be nothing more than a stuffed shirt. In those moments, you need to reach beyond the accepted protocols of society. If the law lets you down, you can turn vigilante or you can turn to the dark arts. I told the damp huddle of suspects that I needed them to stay where they were and to prepare themselves. Cold drinks were handed around to further confuse everyone, whilst Silvia drove out of the compound on a mission I had started to plan whilst I watched the policemen wade through their ineffectual masquerade.

All eyes turned to the gates when the Land Cruiser rolled back into the yard. The conversation and laughter that had filled the space was replaced by an ominous silence. The passenger door swung open and a very large Malawian unfolded himself from the front seat. He carried a goatskin bag and a stout mopane walking staff. The impact of his presence was immediate. A few nervous whispers and the scent of fear that I had anticipated with the arrival of a witchdoctor.

Now, a witchdoctor or sangoma is exactly like any other sort of medical professional, you turn to them when you can't solve your own problem. Teeth like a deck-swab in Nelson's navy? You call the dentist. Arrhythmia like a Ginger Baker drum track? You track down a cardio-thoracic surgeon. The black dog at your heels? You find a psychiatrist or a barman. These specialists trade off their reputations, charge you money and you hope they can fix you, no guarantee though. They are masters of a singular talent. A witchdoctor is much more useful, an authority on wide-ranging topics both metaphysical and concrete, qualified to cure and essentially to curse, which was specifically the talent I wanted to employ. If fear of the law wasn't a deterrent, then why not try fear of something above the law, or below it?

The Malawian ignored the now silent group of staff and asked to see

Shambolic

the room itself. On the way he explained the terms of his contract to me in an impressively sonorous tone.

'I require an advance payment of fifty pula for the initial consultation and any other services I may need to complete at this place.'

He gestured broadly to the compound and continued,

'I require one thousand pula when the money is returned to you.'

This seemed like a very modern approach to securing his services, get the curse now and pay later in easy instalments! I quite literally had nothing to lose.

'Agreed,' I said as we arrived at the room.

The witchdoctor sized the room up and went to work with his bag of tricks. First, he mixed water with some powder stored in a small leather purse. The foul-smelling ochre-coloured paste was spread liberally across the threshold to the room and a few mystical symbols were outlined onto the floor. The suspects loitered nervously outside the room, afraid and curious in equal measure. A visit from the witchdoctor is quite an event on any ordinary working day.

Mr Voodoo slammed the door in their worried faces and began circling the room chanting what might well have been *Old Macdonald had a farm* in Greek for all we knew. His ocean-deep, ebony-rich tones were splendid. Like all of the best vocal performers, it doesn't really matter what the words are, it is how they sound that transfixes an audience. A few grams of the powder were poured into my wallet, watched closely by the faces now pressed against the small window. There was nothing left in there to worry about, just loose change and that unloved Krona note.

Abruptly, he stopped and pulled a cigarette from his breast pocket for a smoke break. It might have detracted from the show but he was wise enough to incorporate the *gwai* in his routine by blowing a cloud of smoke into the open wallet. He was smoking Benson and Hedges ultralight, which struck me as strange. I hadn't imagined that practitioners of the dark arts would be especially health conscious. I wondered if he ate muesli for breakfast? He finished the cigarette and was evidently finished with the room as well because he opened the door and strode out into the yard. The small crowd gathered around the window stepped back as one and I noticed more than one face reflecting primaeval fear.

The witchdoctor paced over to the gaggle of staff who, without prompting, arranged themselves back into a line. As the victim in this crime, the reaction he was eliciting was far more promising than the lacklustre response to the Keystone Cops. The police, of course, don't get a results-based bonus, they just have to show up. The gardeners, still my prime suspects, looked ashen and flighty.

'Do you know me?' boomed the witchdoctor in that hair ruffling tenor of his.

I saw my overlander pal sit bolt upright in surprise, the tone of authority eliciting some subconscious memory of being caught by the headmaster. In response to the question, a few heads nodded. Maybe I had hired a famous witchdoctor? That had to be a good thing, unless he was famous for being useless.

'One of you has stolen what was not yours,' rumbled Maun's very own James Earl Jones, 'and I will force you to return it, even if you do not wish to do so! When you leave here today, you will start to think about the wrong you have done. You will be unable to focus on anything else, your crime will fill your mind day and night!'

The laundry ladies looked especially troubled by the idea of having to think about this day and night. Forget about gossiping, the village bingo and enjoying a good book, chronic guilt was a fulltime job. I had imagined the curse might involve a spare hand growing out of your head but, in retrospect, gnawing internal misery was probably much easier to conjure.

'You will become like a crazed person,' he continued, 'you will find no peace and those around you will know what you have done and shun you!'

He waved his staff about and kicked some dust up like a rooster. Everyone was transfixed, guilty or not.

'The only way to stop this insanity will be to return the stolen money and then I will lift this curse.'

He paced the line, glaring into the faces that dared to meet his gaze, though most of the group had found interesting things on the ground to study.

'How long will this curse last?' asked the sweatiest gardener, driven to voice his concerns despite his question sounding something like an admission of guilt.

The witchdoctor stopped walking, turned to the man and after a dramatic pause, answered, 'Forever!'

I could practically hear the dry swallows as my prime suspects thought about their options. Either return the cash and stay sane or descend into financially secure lunacy. For his finale, the Malawian threw the remaining magic dust into the late morning air before walking back to the Land Cruiser; it seemed that his work was done. The staff broke up into groups and drifted silently away into the compound. Muddy exhaled a puff of bottled tension, 'Sheesh!'

'So when one of these guys turns up acting crazy,' I wanted to check the protocol, 'I should come and find you?'

'They will come within a week and then I will lift the curse!' he confirmed, 'then I will require final payment.'

That was the last time I saw the Malawian, the prime suspects or the money. We went to South Africa for a month and tried to forget all about the miserable experience. One of the tremendous benefits of youth is the ability to move happily on.

In truth, I had almost forgotten the theft when three months later on another visit to Maun, the compound caretaker told me a story that really brought the chapter to a close. The two gardeners had never returned to work, presumably gone off to live the good life with their new found wealth. One of them had gone to Victoria Falls and had been stabbed to death in a bottle store. The second gardener had been arrested in Maun for a separate crime and was now in prison. Karmic retribution had been extremely thorough. Of course, it could have been pure coincidence, but I doubt it.

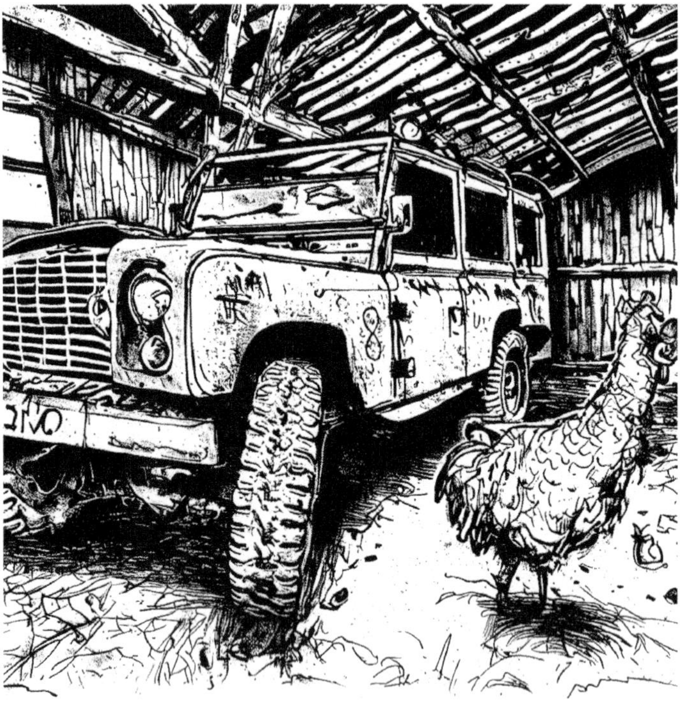

Nomad DeLuxe

Faced with a month of leave and no longer having the funds to rent light aircraft and beach villas, my long-planned luxury surfari was stuffed back into my subconscious. Despite the initial shock of changed circumstances, the lizard brain, that most ancient computer, never tires from problem solving. The Indian Ocean islands were out of reach, but the glorious KwaZul u-Natal coastline offered a budget solution. Access, however, was a problem as there is no public transport in South Africa that takes you anywhere other than city centres. In South Africa you get where you want to go by car. I lived in a safari camp, a self-contained universe with company Land Rovers for ranging across the wilderness, so I had never needed to own a vehicle. That had never been a problem, until now.

As night fell, like a humid funeral shroud over the sorry events of the day, the arrival of a friend delivered the answer. Louis was driving back to Pretoria for his own leave. He could offer a much-needed ride to South Africa and also, if we could get it started, a Series 3 Land Rover with which to explore the golden coast.

I didn't need asking twice and the following morning, Louis, his wife Hoens, Silvia and I were on the road out of Maun. Movement, especially away from the scene of trauma, is like mainlining dopamine. That is why people search for happy anywhere other than the place they are. Like any chemical reward, it is always a short-term fix, but this was better than fighting with the justice system in Maun. We were covering our shortfall

Shambolic

in cash by abusing Silvia's state scholarship from Innsbruck University. Austria has a very generous academic funding programme which, as far as I could tell, had allowed Silvia to travel all over the planet. A surfari underwritten by the Austrian taxpayer? The high alpine farmers of the Tyrol would be apoplectic with impotent rage.

We put our troubles in the rear view mirror and headed south. The long road across the Kalahari is something you can tolerate with enough cigarettes and rock music. Donkeys and children dot the bleak highway at each tiny settlement, before you surge onto another 100 kilometre stretch of sun-baked tarmac. South Africa floods its neighbours with trade goods on this road. Trucks laden with everything from agricultural equipment to cheap plastic garden furniture. That transport route has also been responsible for the import of HIV, shared across truck stops. The worst trade legacy in history. My camp, Maun and most of Botswana in the 1990s was plagued by the disease, a toxic contamination of paradise. Driving south though, against that tide, was as good as forgetting these imperfections for a while.

We cleared the border into South Africa and stopped for the night in Ellisras, a coal mining town. The motel we checked into had a separate bar for ladies, thoughtful in a rough neighbourhood. The door of the ladies bar had a notice nailed up, 'No shorts, T-shirts or firearms inside the bar.' We were gone before first light and the marathon of motoring finally brought us to Louis' family farm, north of Pretoria, on farmland that has been the envy of cattle owners for centuries.

There was a shed on that farm and in that shed was the possible solution to our immediate problem. Louis swung the doors open and we peered into the dusty interior. The Land Rover looked to have all the essential components in place: chassis, engine, seats and a roof. Clearly, the vehicle had been residing in peaceful solitude for some time. A layer of thick dust coated every surface and some old Coke bottles on the floor were half full of dead flies. Miss Havisham wrought from iron, with a homemade bull bar welded onto her tattered wedding dress.

We checked filters, spark plugs, put some clean petrol in, then turned the key which started the vintage four-wheel drive first attempt. No big deal we shrugged, but we were both surprised. I had new models in camp that weren't that reliable and this was a late '70s issue. None of the tyres matched, there was a serious issue with the oil seal on the rear differential and, like all old Land Rovers, it had a collection of DIY upgrades from previous owners, most of which had no obvious purpose.

We rolled out into the sunlight and took a cautious test drive around the property. I'll be honest, the Landy could have caught fire and I would still have opted to go the self-drive route, so strong is the sense of freedom offered by the automobile. I have never liked being a passenger, rigid transport schedules or the inability to choose a compass point and go. Ten hours later and Louis was waving us off down the long track back to the highway. I wonder what he was thinking?

Now we were rolling, nomad deluxe, moving south across the great green swathes of grazing land that had attracted so many opportunists before us. The rich reward discovered by the first great wave of nomadic pastoralists from East Africa on their way to establish mighty kingdoms that would one day bloody the sunburned noses of the colonials. The hunter-gatherer furnace of the Kalahari now far behind us, we were just the latest human drifters searching for long, soft grass and better times. Our slow progress was appraised from hilltops by the cool spirit gaze of Zulu impis, stabbing blades erect like the wind-rattled reeds along the riverbank. You might not actually see them, but you certainly feel them.

The ancient Land Rover topped out just under a hundred kilometres per hour, the modern equivalent of an ox-drawn cart. Two hours into the journey, the speedo cable snapped and then I could only guess at velocity. As we rumbled through the morning traffic heading into Pretoria, the dust started to come loose, along with some of the paint. The pump attendants in the fuel station whistled with appreciation, either because they saw the vehicle as a statement of workers' solidarity or because they thought we were nuts and they liked that. I filled the double long-range tank, which also had a perished seal, so care had to be taken to avoid flooding the footwell with the last couple of litres. The sand-blasted tyres got some air, but I had some doubts about their life expectancy. It would definitely be better if the rain held off for a month. I was glad that South African traffic cops have a flexible approach to vehicle roadworthiness. If you are happy to drive it, good luck to you, brother.

Shambolic

The road to the coast is straightforward, take the N17 out of Pretoria, stay on it until you cross into KwaZulu-Natal and keep going until you hit the beach. We drove through endless farming dorps, blind to their charms beyond fuel and food, fixated on warm waves and ocean breezes. That old Landy left rust and mysterious chunks of iron on the high streets of Ermelo and Piet Retief but we weren't stopping. I was channelling Dean Moriarty on his epic race across the USA, cigarettes on the dashboard and a cool blonde in the passenger seat. That said, the Series 3 wasn't entirely on-board with my crusade. Second gear had stopped working early in the day and any attempt to force it into action just resulted in the sound of tortured metal as the gear lever kicked like a piston. That was okay, you can get by with three gears on empty roads. The rear differential seal was a bigger problem, it leaked a near continual drip of oil when the engine was running. Every fuel stop meant a top-up, bad for the environment, pretty bad for anyone following us on a motorbike and, eventually, almost terminal for the trip.

The brakes were exactly what I had expected, they had more of a theoretical than practical application. To stop, you needed warning and time to start pumping some pressure into the air-filled system. Those old pipes contained more bubbles than a warm bottle of champagne. I usually started to shed speed about 500 metres before any obstacles; stationary traffic, children playing in the road, livestock and small towns. At one small town's four-way stop, the brakes didn't respond and I had to drive up a wide clay bank to blast around the huddle of local traffic waiting at the junction. I didn't drop my cigarette either. Dean would have been proud.

We were being overtaken by the majority of other road users, but having a full month at your disposal removes any serious need for speed. That and the fact that our to-do list read:

1. Drive to the beach.
2. Surf.

Our four-wheel environmental catastrophe kept rolling on, leaving small birds choking in our wake and a slick of vital motor lubricants across the tarmac. The first serious geographical challenge arose in the shape of the Pongola Mountain pass. This is where you leave Mpumalanga behind and head into KwaZulu-Natal. If Hannibal could coax his elephants over the Alps and Alexander his great army across the Hindu Kush, surely we could force our aged chariot over a lowly tarred mountain road?

The climb was borderline motoring comedy as we crawled up the pass, slipstreaming donkey carts and wrinkled old cyclists to gain an edge. This is where second gear is traditionally helpful. Instead, I crunched between first and glorious, but typically brief, spurts of third gear. Local families came out of their homes to watch what they thought was a vintage car rally. We took it in turns to climb out and stretch our legs beside the Landy. Once we both got out to amble beside the four-wheel drive as it chugged along in first gear, bouncing between potholes. After a considerable amount of time, patience and fuel had been depleted, we reached the summit. The shimmering lake and lush nature reserve spread out below us. I had a feeling my hands would be occupied for the coming descent, so I lit a cigarette in preparation and let the smooth tyres roll over the crest.

The uphill crawl was quickly forgotten as the Landy began to barrel down the mountain, gravity in the driving seat. I knew we had a decent head of steam because we started to overtake the buses that had roared past us in our previous slow lane lives. I had no real plan for emergency stopping other than engaging reverse gear and assuming the brace position. Children screamed and drivers gasped as we veered around traffic and squeezed through impossible gaps. The alien velocity generated so much excess current through the alternator that the few electrical systems still working began to self-operate. The windscreen wipers flailed madly as they tried to keep pace with their super-charged motors. The indicators flashed a mad morse code of their own. If we had a tape player it would have been spinning at Mickey Mouse speed.

A peculiar vibration took hold of the aged steel frame and bolts began falling out of the canopy. Things were literally falling apart. The traditionally vague steering built into each and every pre-1995 Land Rover meant that I could just about follow the tarred road, but not always in the correct lane. We wandered into the uphill lane a few times and fought to return to neutral territory before the next truck flashed past. Somehow we reached the base of the hill alive. The Series 3 was bouncing over any surface imperfections it met like a lively but demented puppy. It took a full two kilometres to regain normal cruising speed alongside the Pongola Dam.

I can't remember what we talked about on that surprisingly rapid journey, but the stressed engine was wheezing like a retired coal miner when I pulled over for another smoke.

Off the Road

Our automotive K2 conquered, nothing stood between us and the Indian Ocean. It was going to be surf wax and sun tanning from here on in. Two hundred kilometres or so to St Lucia which had become our destination of choice for no reason other than having a name we liked. The hours and remaining light ran by, the green landscape ripe with possibilities. We had enough time to make it to St Lucia before needing to deploy what I guessed would be pathetic headlights.

As I rounded a corner and spotted the rusted sign for Hluhluwe, the largest pothole in Kwazulu-Natal filled the road ahead like some ancient sinkhole. If I'd had functioning brakes I probably would have stopped. However, I didn't, so we just braced for impact. That foul crater launched the tired Landy a couple of feet into the soft evening breeze, clear air beneath her spinning wheels like the Dukes of Hazzard on safari. We thumped into the road on the far side of the chasm, leaving a million rust particles to drift into a melancholy pile in our wake. I gripped the wheel and waited, the vehicle was going to self-diagnose the extent of her injuries sooner or later. Five seconds, ten… nothing, perhaps we had gotten away with it.

I felt it would be prudent to pull over and give the vehicle a quick once over just for the sake of curiosity. The usually springy brake pedal went hard to the floor and stayed there; clearly we were lacking the essential fluid required to return the pedal and slow the Landy. Air brakes work fine in vehicles fitted with them but the Series 3 Land Rover wasn't one of those.

'The brakes are gone,' I mentioned to Silvia.

'Don't worry, we are almost there,' came the beatific reply from someone who hadn't yet driven the Landy and wasn't especially interested in its mechanical workings.

I wanted to have my companion understand what I was going through, in apparent isolation on the right-hand side of the vehicle. Silvia decided that coasting to the beach and parking up a hill would be enough for now. The Bushlands turnoff loomed.

As it was uphill, I pulled onto it hoping the gradient would stop us before we reached the top and got t-boned by a local cattle truck. That worked fine and I left the Landy in 1st gear while I climbed out, expecting to find a disconnected brake fluid pipe dripping from the undercarriage. Instead, I tripped over the back right tyre which had made a break for freedom, along with the side shaft, wrenched from its natural habitat in the rear differential.

'Shit!' I said to nobody in particular.

The Landy was trying to morph into a radical new tri-wheel model. Ever diminishing returns.

The other problem we had was the falling evening gloom. We hadn't passed a house for a good ten minutes, we lacked a mobile 'phone or anyone in the neighbourhood to call even if we had one. This part of South Africa is known for its robberies, shootings and general gangster-liness, just like the rest of the country. Leaving the vehicle would possibly mean losing our belongings and maybe even our stricken ride. I couldn't handle two stick-ups in one month.

Taking a tip from those intelligent creatures in the Kalahari, the meerkats, I went to the highest point available to scan for threats and solutions. Standing on the dented roof, I could just make out the peak of an A-frame house in the woodland half a kilometre away. On consideration, it seemed safer for Silvia to walk to the house than to stand by the open road under a neon victim sign. I sat on the bonnet and twirled a tyre iron, like a comfort blanket. After ten minutes, I pictured my girlfriend arriving at a remote house halfway through the local Satanists' convention, during a seminar entitled, 'Human offerings and the disposal of their remains.' The long drive and adrenaline decline were having an effect in the clammy near dark.

Then an engine started, faint through the trees and headlights approached, winding along a dirt track. A Toyota double-cab came into view, driving the wrong way on the off-ramp hard shoulder. It reminded me of a T-shirt I'd seen, boldly stating 'I'd rather push my Land Rover than drive your Toyota.' Well, the engineering of the rising sun looked pretty good to me. In a stroke of pure dumb serendipity, we had broken down in front of the local cop's house. He had come prepared with his 9mm handgun stuffed in his jeans and didn't look professionally impressed with my tyre iron health insurance policy. We now had a local friend with genuinely useful contacts.

He called out the cop shop tow truck to haul our vehicle to his plot. We drank beer on the bull bar whilst we waited, the sheriff entertaining us with stories of pensioners being shot for pocket change and weekly carjackings on that same stretch of road. South Africans love to discuss national crime rates and South African cops love the bloody details. On beer two, he explained that he was quitting the force to join one of those pyramid sales schemes. In his opinion, the modern police were corrupt and ineffective. A superb morale booster for any self-drive tourist in the country.

The tow truck lumbered out of the dark, a Nissan, and the mechanic climbed out, shook his head knowingly and muttered, 'Focken' Land Rover!'

He clearly had a high opinion of this iconic piece of British engineering.

'If it wasn't for these focken' shite Land Rovers, I'd have been out of business years ago. I focken' love 'em!'

Since I was standing next to a four-wheel drive vehicle with only three wheels, I wasn't in a very strong position to defend the venerable brand. We managed to hammer the side shaft and tyre back into place and slowly towed the hulk back to the cop's house. The mechanic discovered that the bearing had been deprived of grease for at least a decade and had essentially welded itself onto the shaft around which it was meant to spin. He said he would be back in the morning to see if he could improve our chances of reaching the Indian Ocean that month.

We were stranded for two days, enjoying the hospitality of the cop and his extended family. Silvia entertained the children and I offered semi-professional encouragement to a brother-in-law about to build his own tented camp in Hluhluwe. The mechanic and his grease monkeys struggled to get the seized bearings out and new ones in. Every component that was meant to be coated in lovely grease was as dry as a mummified stick insect. The oil from the rear differential fell out in a solid rubber block, robbed of its viscous qualities by time and abuse.

As he worked, the mechanic offered many pieces of advice on how to proceed with a vehicle in this condition. He was sure the shaft would detach again at some point and cautioned a top speed of fifty kilometres per hour. Anything faster would certainly result in injury or death to passengers and nearby pedestrians. He had me tell him again about the drive over the Pongola Pass, which he translated into isiZulu for the amusement of his crew. Heads shook and they whistled in mock amazement. These fellows would happily clamber into a death trap minibus taxi with thirty occupants and no headlights or brakes, but ride in this Land Rover? Are you nuts!

On day three of our unplanned diversion, he said there was nothing more he could do and we paid over two weeks' worth of food money. As he climbed into his Nissan for the last time, our mechanic mentioned that the engine also sounded duff, before pulling away in a cloud of dust.

That night, we bought steak for our generous hosts and enjoyed a sociable braai, swapping contact details that, as more often than not, were never going to be used. We were just transients, passing through, lucky to have met the best possible people in a pinch.

If I had known then that our chariot had more mechanical thrills and spills in store, I would have dumped it back on the highway as a poisoned gift to the criminal fraternity.

Flotsam and Jetsam and Bliksem

A couple of uneventful hours later, salt tangible in the warm air, we reached the outskirts of Richard's Bay. Freight and shipping is what brings most people to this low-rise town, squatting beside the brilliant blue of the Indian Ocean. It was hard to tell if the town's star was in its ascendant or a leisurely sun-bleached decline. We sat outside the Richard's Bay Yacht Club and ate lunch whilst studying our map. The view was an oily wharf lined with tugboats; it wasn't obvious where the yachts were. The only reason we had stopped there was to find a surfboard before heading up the coast towards Mozambique. The waiter supplied directions to what he said was the only surf shop in town.

This was in a row of tired looking outlets on the beachfront, overlooking a couple of industrial breakwaters. Every cool kid in town seemed to have skipped school to hang around outside the gloomy little enterprise. There was a tuneless guitar being murdered on the pavement and the usual endless adolescent search for another cigarette. Their lament could have been the chorus, 'Hey bru, spare a *gwaai*?' A decade or so younger and I would have been right there with them, staring at the waves and talking about the endless summer to come after school days were done. I was broke, but not as broke as they were.

The kid behind the counter looked genuinely surprised that he had a customer who wasn't just trying to borrow a lighter or some surf wax. The sun had burned him such a deep copper that he looked like a sculpture. The little store was empty, clearly the beach crowd stuck to the pavement where life was free and nobody expected you to part with money. One wall had a row of second-hand boards arranged in an untidy line-up. They ranged from a thruster missing a fin, to an ancient single fin that looked like a bowling ball had been bounced on it for a while.

The kid was anxious to persuade us with his snappy surf speak and sales patter.

'Howzit, my bru?'

His greeting was delivered with a sunny smile.

'Coaster!'

My beach slang return volley scored a genuine grin and he pointed to the rack.

'This board is kief!'

He enthusiastically selected a crooked piece of fibreglass that looked partially melted. Despite his efforts to steer us towards a couple of design dogs, I pulled out a decent mini-mal that was tucked into the back corner. It was the only board in the store that looked like it retained some buoyancy and I could see by the shaper's brand that it had been made for the local waves.

The salesman looked slightly sad and I suspected he had been saving that one for himself, a perk of the job. Despite his initial dismay, he rallied and asked for six hundred rand. In Europe, that is essentially giving a hand-shaped board away for free and I felt some shame for out-manoeuvring the village idiot. In Richard's Bay, he thought I was a sucker for not haggling over the price. Everyone was happy!

On our way out of town we pulled into a fuel station to fill the Landy's tanks. The pump attendant had filled about half of the main tank when he was soaked from the waist down by petrol.

'Bliksem!'

The shocked youngster dropped the fuel nozzle and ran. Another seal had perished and with it, the ability to separate fuel from driver and the surrounding environment. I couldn't be bothered to retreat, but it did seem likely we were about to be blown into low space orbit by this cursed transport. The petrol dripped, the chemical slick spread but nothing ignited. The attendant cautiously returned to throw sand across the spill. I went to pay for the fuel whilst the spillage evaporated under the early afternoon sun. The huge cashier, dressed like Shaka Zulu for some promotion or other, leaned out from his window and said, 'Focken' Land Rover!'

As the late afternoon light burnished KwaZulu-Natal golden, shadows grew across the road and we pulled into St Lucia. The town was closing down for winter, more in accordance with the international protocols of small coastal resorts than any climatic factors. I love unfashionable beach towns, they don't pretend to be anything other than a gathering of people sharing relaxed anonymity. It is warm all year here and the beaches are beautiful. Seasons are undoubtedly a sales and marketing distraction. The small hotel we found had thirty rooms and we could choose from twenty-eight as two were being painted, the owner said, before asking why we smelt of petrol.

We hauled our luggage into the room and set out for the beach. Turning right onto the main street, the tortured gearbox began a percussive clunk… clunk… clunk and the gear lever went limp. There is a popular phrase in the Arab world, 'A thousand curses never tore a shirt.' If you embellish the curses with kicking and punching though, you can definitely add some dents to the bodywork.

I trudged back along the road to find an open garage and considered the economic logic of persisting with this fool's errand. The Land Rover clearly missed its natural habitat, dust caked in that peaceful barn, enjoying quiet companionship with the mice and bats. Safari camps are exactly like that old Landy, full of hope but fundamentally flawed by both the humans that operate them and the equipment we push beyond the limits of reason. This was a rich man's vehicle, it needed a support team and ideally someone machining spare parts as and when required. Instead, I paid a grinning local mechanic another wedge of cash to revive the patient once again; how often can Lazarus rise anyway?

Silvia and I sat in the fume-filled cab, discussing finances, our available time and whether we could actually afford to start the vehicle and attempt forward motion again. It would probably have been cheaper to rent a Ferrari in Johannesburg at the start of the trip but youth always beats pure logic so I turned the key, one last roll of the dice. It was too late to surf anyway, so we drove slowly back to the hotel to track down an early dinner.

I'll be honest, the derelict-chic of back street St Lucia wasn't lacking in charm. Vines grew along telegraph poles, properties were unfenced, flip flops were de rigueur and I didn't have to think about the camp. Cold beer and grilled kingklip in the dusky embrace of the evening wasn't a consolation prize, they were the reason we were drifting. Our original plan had been an extended tour of the coast, hunting out backwaters en route to Durban for a decent bunny chow before heading back to Botswana. As things stood with our rubber-shod companion, I redrew our effective range of exploration to sixty kilometres from that spot. Not so much the world is an oyster, as our world was now the size of an oyster. That concession gave us a shot at getting back to Pretoria as a threesome. As the coast of KwaZulu-Natal is really just a continuous stretch of golden beach, a stone's throw in any direction was still a prize-winner.

A brand-new day broke, filled with promise and very low expectations regarding the auto. This stretch of coastline has forest and dune-anchoring grasses growing right to the high tide mark. The Indian Ocean is warm and exotic as all naturally heated environments are to Europeans. In colder climes, families will endure sand-blasting at the beach as soon as our life-giving star hints at an appearance. Day after day of perfect beach weather is just a fairytale told by grandparents to unbelieving grandchildren. On this blessed shoreline though, it is reality, which makes the behaviour of the locals all the more confusing.

A prevalence of four-wheel drives and vehicle access to the shoreline has resulted in an odd petrol-head beach culture. The last place I wanted the Landy to croak was axle-deep in warm sand, I did enough of that in my day job. So we parked up in the shade and hiked down to the beach. As pedestrians, we were as unusual on that stretch of sand as an ATM in the Makgadikgadi Pans. Dune buggies blasted down the wet sand and families from Gauteng in new four-wheel drives chewed through the dunes, all festooned with fishing rods, looking like fallen satellites. Perfectly tuned machines, perfectly out of tune with nature.

We perched on the crest of a dune and studied this behaviour. An ancestral link to times when being self-sufficient and self-propelled made the difference between success and failure, like Persian charioteers thundering across the plains to introduce unfortunate infantry to the future.

One family pulled up below us, turned their double cab for a decent view of the backlit waves and parked. They ate their lunch in the vehicle and then drove away, never having set foot on the sand. We felt like hunter-gathers in this company. Drivers would slow to shout greetings and share information, there is civility amongst the like-minded in all places.

'Anywhere good to drive up there?'

'Ja! We drove all the way to Black Rock. Tourist guide says it takes forty minutes but we did it in thirty, eh love?'

His wife, nodding with pride.

'Lekker. Watch out for the idiots walking on the beach though, we almost hit some guy with a surfboard coming out of the sea!'

'No!'

'True, bloody pedestrians...'

Then they'd crank their turbos and drive over egg-laying leatherback

Shambolic

turtles and sunbathers all the way back to the tar road.

Swimming seemed to be very low on the list of beach activities around St Lucia, maybe it was the sharks or the strong currents that dissuaded the motorists? Living in the Okavango Delta where work and play typically brings you into close contact with some of nature's most proficient killers tends to reset the bar on acceptable risk. We swam everywhere, diving through the shore break to drift in the powerful embrace of the water, laughing about sharks whilst we floated through their hunting grounds. Silvia was a true believer in Fortuna and I suppose I'm naturally optimistic about the great tumbling dice. Rather a magnificent beast from the deep than a badly driven off road vehicle on the beach. Finally, a concerned resident pulled up as we emerged dripping and energised from the ocean.

'You folks need to swim at Cape Vidal,' he shouted over the pounding surf, 'the lagoon there is safe!'

He gave a cheery wave, a knowing shake of the head and floored his buggy up the sand.

We consulted the map and, sure enough, Cape Vidal was within my designated 'can do' range, accessed through land managed by the Parks Board. The owner of the hotel agreed with the advice and, ever considerate of motoring requirements, added, 'Good road as well, solid!'

So three days after we had limped into town, we threw our toys into the Landy, collected a picnic and headed up the coast. The first hundred yards of track were beautiful soft sand which we drifted across, then the wheels rolled onto the corrugated surface that ran the rest of the way to the Cape. These heavily ridged calcrete tracks are standard stuff across Africa, literally the crests of static waves in the road. In a four-wheel drive you just speed up to skim across them and let some air out of your tyres if you want real luxury. Modern suspension makes all but the worst corrugations imperceptible, but not so the ancient hulk of the Series 3.

Initially, the chassis started to make a high-speed percussive vibration which reminded me a lot of Gene Kruppa on the snare drum. It swelled to a deafening drone as the metal bodywork and fibreglass canopy competed for tonal superiority. I floored the accelerator in a bid to find that mystical sweet spot of velocity that would silence what was becoming a mobile drum kit. It got louder and harder to hold a course as the vague steering failed to interpret the madly skipping tyres. I also wondered about the life expectancy of that back right wheel.

Slowing brought the cacophony into almost bearable audible range but increased the vibration through the metalwork. Silvia had fingers in her ears and watched as the nuts began to spin from the canopy bolts and fall into the footwell. Dust danced like a whirling dervish across the sun-bleached dashboard. 'Fuuuuck!' was the only intelligent comment I could utter with a Marlboro clamped between my teeth. After ten minutes of punishment, I coasted to a stop just so we could regain our senses. We sat in dazed silence, hearing dulled, staring ahead at the road stretching away from us, kilometre after corrugated kilometre.

'Knock! Knock!'

I turned to Silvia but she didn't appear to be moving her lips.

'Knock! Knock!'

I looked right and met a cheerful face peering into the cab. A woman walking beside the trail had noticed our vehicle, pointing in the right direction and blessed with empty seating in the back. A gift on a hot walk with bags to carry home.

'Cape Vidal?' she queried.

'That's it,' I replied although my voice sounded faint through my own suppressed hearing, 'want a ride?'

As I offered the lift, I did wonder if I should add some sort of passenger warning based on our experience. The lady laughed and climbed into the back, settling on the narrow metal bench, which some long-dead design engineer had felt fulfilled his brief for *additional seating*.

'Alright, let's go!' I said to nobody in particular as we clicked into first gear and built up some speed for the jump to third. I turned to check on our passenger and noticed the smile had been replaced by a look of growing consternation. She was trying to maintain her position by wedging her legs across the cargo bay floor and seemed to be even more in synchronisation with the vibrating frame than we were in our slightly padded seats. Her great bosom was behaving like the harmonic sound waves you see on those oscillating machines in physics class. I was seeing double by now, but our vehicle had clearly become a stress

Shambolic

and strain experiment.

Another ten minutes of abuse and I cut the engine before round three. As I reached for the pack of cigarettes that had been hurled onto the floor like anything else not screwed down, the back door opened and slammed.

'Ngiyabonga!'

The well-shaken lady offered conciliatory thanks as she hurried to put distance between herself and her tormentor. Imagine preferring to walk in the midday heat rather than ride in a pre-modern conveyance; that is a damning review of the Series 3.

We didn't have the option of walking away. So, after two shell shocked hours, we found the deep sandy track winding down to the shore at Cape Vidal. The shady parking area beside the Parks Board hut was almost empty, just a combi van and a couple of two-wheel drive cars. There was a sign saying, 'Vehicle access to beach requires a permit,' and the track beyond was a series of deep ruts. A man in these environs without a beach driving permit isn't really a man. A man who gets his vehicle stuck on the beach is probably from Jo'burg. What did that make me exactly? A man with a four-wheel drive which couldn't be trusted off the main drag, or on it for that matter. Despite sand being my stock in trade in the Savuti, I was going to walk.

There was still entertainment to be had, though, as we hiked down and out of the coastal forest. Such as a fresh out of the box Discovery four-wheel drive buried to both axles in the fine warm sand. The Gauteng Province number plate sitting level with the unforgiving material that was trying to swallow it. The owner was huffing about his investment with a face the colour of raw beetroot, clearly enjoying his beach holiday. Harsh words were being bandied about in the way mortals typically communicate their misfortunes to higher beings.

An idea clearly struck the explorer as he suddenly stumbled to the front of his vehicle and began slowly pulling cable and d-bolt from his winch, chuffed that he had got that optional extra at the dealers. He waved the cable end happily at his wife, sitting patiently inside the air-conditioned cab. Problem solved, out of here in a tick my dear! I left him casting increasingly bleak looks around the beach in search of something solid to which he could attach his self-rescue equipment. As we made our way down to the lagoon edge, the gentle onshore breeze and bird calls couldn't quite smother that forlorn wail from above, 'Foooock!' He couldn't have known on that calm afternoon that the gods were already readying their reply to the challenge.

Cape Vidal is as rewardingly lovely as any relatively undisturbed piece of that coastline should be. The exposed rock pools at low tide are full of tropical miracles, like the bonsai gardens of the ocean. It was low season and there were very few people snorkelling or poking around the rock beds. There is a launch point for boats which had a fishing skiff pulled up, waiting for the trailer to haul it off the beach. In the stern sat an elderly man, smoking a hand-rolled cigarette in happy solitude.

'Catch?' I called over and he beckoned me across the sand, a beatific smile on his face that I knew from my own fishing trips. Looking over the side, I saw he had a big male dorado at his feet, an incredible fish up close, with an enormous blunt forehead, iridescent blues, green and gold across the strong body. The colours were starting to fade, greying as living energy left the fish, perhaps going nowhere other than into the body of the old fisherman. I whistled in appreciation because a fish like that deserves some respect.

'You fish?' he asked without taking his eyes, alive with evident delight, from his catch.

'Fly,' I said, 'mostly tigers.'

I lit my own cigarette because that is what we both wanted to do, smoke and look at the dorado in piscatorial satisfaction.

'Fly?' the eyes raised and he cocked his tanned face like a further question.

His eyes flicked to the rod rack and he nodded encouragement for me to follow the gaze.

I turned and saw a row of powerful saltwater rods, standard stuff on the coast and about as subtle as a harpoon gun. Then, on the extreme left, the unmistakably slender profile of a fly rod, still rigged with a lure. I was honestly humbled, the chances of success against a rod-breaking predator like the dorado on a fragile fly rig? No need to ask questions about the fight. I'd lost scores of river fish to their sudden blasts of impossible energy, my equipment failing to match up to nature. Looking back at the contented face beside me, he nodded again, pleased by my recognition of a rare talent.

Further up the beach, his companion with the boat trailer had stopped to help the emotionally shattered disco-driver. Silvia was waving, excited by something in a rock pool, not excited about the boat and the old guy.

'Incredible!' I offered in parting and his eyes fell back to the great fish beside him.

Half an hour later, the boat blasted past us behind a battered Land Cruiser as the epic tale made its way back to some bar in St Lucia. We were passing Mission Rock, halfway home and I was driving the Landy flat out to compress the discomfort of the corrugated road.

Then the sky broke, a single deafening crash, a lance of lightning which lit the road like a million-watt spotlight and a torrent of warm rain. In seconds, the deluge was trickling through the many empty bolt holes in the canopy and running down the inside of the windscreen. In conditions like that, the windscreen wipers were simply ornamental, ineffectually smearing water across the glass. I took my T-shirt off to use as an interior wiper and kept my foot hard on the floor. We were only doing about fifty kilometres per hour.

Then we hit the edge of town and we were suddenly doing sixty on the smooth tar, aquaplaning down the main street on our racing-slick tyres. Restaurant owners were pulling down shutters and retrieving plastic chairs that had tumbled into the street. The hotel had a cement canopy above the entrance and I pulled up in its cover where we sat and watched the road turn into a shallow stream before our eyes. This was the leading edge of a cyclonic storm system blowing down from Mozambique, where it had battered Maputo to pieces, according to the excited weatherman on the local news. The rain lasted for an entire week and resulted in nine metre swells breaking onto the Durban waterfront.

If heaven is going to rain on your parade, at least make the storm a biblical one!

Ben Forbes

Crap Taxidermy

St Lucia, like most beach towns, doesn't really offer much indoor entertainment. Once we got bored of drinking beer, sleeping late and watching television, we headed for the local crocodile farm. A bit of a busman's holiday, considering we lived in one of Africa's largest natural reptile habitats. This particular tourist attraction was created by what used to be known as the Natal Parks Board. It was pretty obvious that bad weather was the best kind of weather for the farm. Families ran from vehicles to the shelter offered by thatched buildings dotted around the sandy car park.

The first rondavel we ducked into held a collection of display cases that were home to stuffed exhibits in varying states of decay. Some of them may have once been living creatures but, in the gloomy half-light, it was difficult to tell. Plastic eyes had fallen out, seams had sprung to bleed stuffing and, in a few extreme cases, body parts had fallen off. It looked as though these unfortunate reptiles had been euthanized with a grenade and left where they fell. Like all nature exhibits, there were information boards attached to each scene. They talked about interesting crocodilian facts, of which there are many, this is a surviving representative of the great age of dinosaurs after all. It would have been funnier if they had just declared visual reality. Sad little crocodile, three legs. Crocodile nest diorama, made from ping pong balls. Crocodile with small plastic shark in mouth.

The rain slackened and we stepped back onto the pathway outside. This led to something looking like a shipwreck victim's homemade escape craft. It was a timber raft, random planking bound to a hull of ancient two hundred litre fuel drums. A thick metal chain with an evil hook attached trailed from the raft like a bizarre fishing device. It could have been the work of a demented carpentry class in some very remote school. The exhibit lacked any explanation but, as we stood and discussed the point of the contraption, a Parks Board employee wandered past. He was in overalls, not a tour guide, more of a groundsman, but he stopped when I waved at him.

'Do you know what this is all about?' I asked.

Shambolic

'Oh yes,' he looked upon the raft with a knowing smile, 'this is for catching sharks!'

'Sharks?'

I wasn't seeing an obvious connection.

'Or crocodiles maybe?' He thought about that for a second, 'sharks *and* crocodiles,' he affirmed.

I looked back at the rig and pointed to the chain. 'You bait that hook?' It seemed logical.

'Oh yes,' he nodded, happy we were all on the same page. 'You put the dog there!'

'Dog?' that seemed very specific, 'why does it have to be a dog? Sharks eat fish as well?'

He looked at me with a pitying glance, clearly disturbed that I wasn't keeping up.

'No, the dog must swim, splash, splash!' he mimed a couple of doggy paddles for us.

Silvia groaned in European animal loving dismay.

'You put a live dog on the hook?'

At the risk of labouring a simple point of shark fishing etiquette, I wanted to get this madness straight. Our piscatorial expert exhaled a breath, his patience tested.

'You take this raft out in the sea,' he pointed towards the beach for emphasis, 'then put a dog on the hook.'

He lifted the chain and rusted hook to illustrate how the unfortunate mutt might be secured through its back.

'Then you throw him in the water and he will swim towards the beach, very fast, much splashing in the water.'

Silvia had walked away from the grim tale but I couldn't leave, transfixed by the mediaeval simplicity of the concept.

'The shark comes to see and eats the dog.'

'Then he is caught on the hook and the raft keeps him from escaping?'

I finished the plot and was rewarded with a nod of pleasure, now I was getting it, not quite as dumb as I looked. It still sounded a little far-fetched to me, even for Africa.

'You've tried this?'

'Oh, no!' This answer came with a furtive glance around that suggested the opposite, 'this is illegal, only for poachers!'

Then my cultural tutor headed back the way he had come, whistling softly and leaving me to consider the horrific final moments of the stray canine. I caught up with Silvia alongside an enclosed pond containing a Nile crocodile half submerged in the slimy water. She was regarding the lone inhabitant with dismay, the leviathan returning the sentiment.

It was time to go. This emotional low point on the golden coast made it easier to head home to Botswana. As the sun rose over the nervous street dogs of St Lucia, we were already several hours into the drive back north.

Incredibly, the return journey went without any serious vehicular incidents. The leaking rear differential needed topping up at every fuel stop, like a choleric infant being fed a soothing snake oil. Eventually we rumbled into the suburbs of Johannesburg and an overnight stay with a cousin. I suffered a malaria relapse, nothing as dramatic as the original dose the month before, just hours lost in fever dreams. It is hard to describe the physical sensations rising from malaria, because it is hard to remember anything at all. It feels like a sleeping pill that only delivers bad dreams and wakes you for brief semi-lucid moments of extreme chills or pouring sweat.

Whilst I white-knuckled the fever spikes, Silvia took the Landy to the local shopping mall to collect some supplies. Lacking the many hours of familiarity I had won at the slightly loose steering wheel, she discovered for herself how little the brakes responded at the first set of traffic lights. Using logic under pressure, she chose the smallest Japanese car on the road to fulfil the role of surrogate brake. This left a bullbar-shaped dent in the back of the tiny commuter which, as she described, had 'been in the way.' Fake names and addresses were swapped, Silvia drove slowly back to the house and stated that she would never drive the old four-wheel drive again.

That is why I found myself hunched over the steering wheel in early morning Pretoria traffic, when I should have been in a hospital being given morphine and other fine things. In my depleted state, we became hopelessly lost. It felt like part of some great conspiracy in my altered

Shambolic

state. My mind was definitely playing tricks on me as I fought to resurrect some of my crushed energy, hoping for enough to just reach the farm.

Eventually, I pulled into a fuel station and refused to leave the vehicle. I fumbled with an unlit cigarette whilst Silvia went to ask for directions. By the time she returned, my sweaty hands had soaked through the thin stick of tobacco and it had disintegrated into two sodden pieces. Things are bleak when you can't even smoke a cigarette in your own company. A newspaper hawker wandered over from the main road to stare in through the window, looking as bad as I felt. We stared at one another, lost souls on the great revolving planet, until the spell was broken by Silvia's return.

The door slammed, reality of sorts and some directions drawn on a piece of cardboard, pictograph-GPS. The lines on the hand-drawn map were strangely comforting, like advice from a good shepherd. One way or another, we followed that cardboard back to the Land Rover's home.

Louis came out onto the farmhouse *stoep* to greet us, or rather Silvia, because I collapsed onto the nearest flat surface and slept for ten hours. When I shook off the last of the malaise, the portable antique had been rolled back into the barn and the doors were shut on an era of motoring best forgotten.

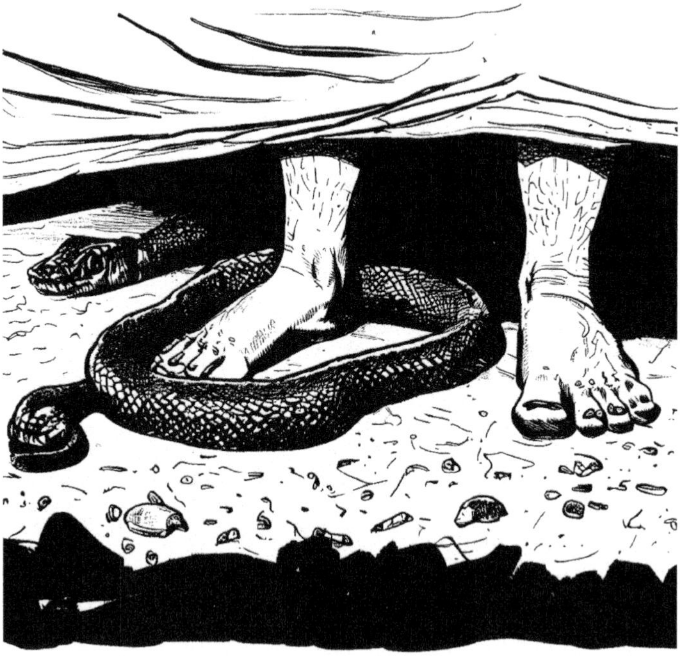

Bloody Wars, Dread Diseases and Bureaucracy

The year 1999 was a massive one for enthusiastic followers of the Gregorian calendar for whom millennia are especially exciting. Technophiles spoke of kiloyears and debated the possible crash of the computer-verse. True believers wondered if this new millennium was *the* millennium they had been waiting for since the Book of Revelation. Conspiracy theorists and other cave dwellers were busy chorusing the end of the world, their favourite tune. I was completely disconnected from human society that New Year's Eve, babysitting an empty camp on the Linyanti River.

It felt just like any Saturday and in truth, the day of the week didn't concern me. What I was concerned about was the serpent we had discovered coiled, silent and menacing, beneath the bed in our tent.

In an empty safari camp, graced with long hot days of complete freedom, I had begun New Year's Eve morning with an attempt at watercolour painting, but it wasn't going well. Silvia was in the tent searching for the mouse she said had woken her in the night, rustling under the bed. As I daubed paint on paper, I thought about that word *rustle* which you don't normally associate with mice. They nibble things, scratch things and tap their dinky little claws on the floor. Silvia was now on the floor of the tent, peering under the bed to find the rustling mouse. If there had been a mouse under there in the night, it had probably been eaten

Shambolic

by the bloody great snake which she discovered in the gloom.

The art class was interrupted by the arrival of my companion, spilling out through the unzipped tent flaps and only halting at a safe distance from the tent.

'Snake!' she pointed back at the tent, with the indignant, accusatory finger, as old as time, with which all humans point out their greatest fears. Snake just means monster, demon, witch, dragon, harpy and anything else you don't want under your bed. I am not a hater of snakes and, if you build a safari camp which is essentially a soft play area for reptiles, you shouldn't be surprised when they come to check out the amusements. That said, I am also a lover of life, compared to say, an excruciatingly painful death in remotest Botswana.

Silvia couldn't offer much detail on the type of snake we had bunking with; it was big, bad and under the bed. I immediately decided that one of my early resolutions for the glorious new year was to avoid being bitten by a serpent. I had a snake stick in the camp office, a simple spring-loaded clamp which could trap and lift the offending demon from its hiding place and relocate it to a more suitable habitat. Like your neighbour's shower, for example.

Armed with my device, I edged back into the tent, checking carefully along the sides of the floor to make sure the devil worm hadn't moved into a new ambush spot. All was clear, so I knelt as far from the bed as I could to look into the slab of darkness beneath. Two demilunes of coil protruded into the sunlight, sleek, grey and unmistakably belonging to a black mamba. The paler grey meant the snake could be a juvenile, which really just means a slightly shorter version of Africa's most venomous snake. The back of my neck prickled with unnatural heat. The most ancient part of my brain, the part we share with our most distant ancestors, fired off fight or flight requests at random. Only dumb curiosity kept me on the spot whilst I considered the immediate options.

We had no access to either antivenom or medical help in the few hours it would probably take for me to succumb to cardiovascular collapse. The snake stick suddenly felt like a plastic spoon at a knife fight. Retreat, then. I slowly backed out of the tent, into the sunshine and security. Silvia was still three metres away in her self-ordained safe zone, probably the smartest move either of us was going to make in the next half an hour. Natural selection at work; good luck and knowing when to duck.

I glanced at the snake stick before dropping it on the table and heading back to the office for a bigger boat. Fortunately for me, the camp was unusually well stocked with firearms, no small thing in a country notoriously stingy with permits for weapons. This is actually a sound protocol, you give people guns and they just run around shooting the wildlife. Anyway, the gun safe contained a .22 rifle with a scope, a single barrel shotgun and a .375 rifle. I instinctively picked the shotgun; this wasn't six-shooters at the OK corral, I wanted an easy win.

Back at the tent, the snake hadn't moved and I started to have a change of heart. It seemed unsporting to blast the poor bugger whilst he slumbered in the morning heat, more of an assassination than a man versus beast death-match. My lizard brain was being tricked by some ridiculous code of honour that modern humans imagine existed on battlefields in the mists of time. I bet knights in well-oiled, shining armour loved sneaking up on their enemies and lancing them whilst they darned their chain mail. There is, however, another alternative to lead in these situations.

I picked up a fly-rod tube, a solid piece of plastic with a sealed end. The idea is to slowly push the tube up to the offending snake and hope that the nice, dark interior seems like a safer place to hide than under your bed. Then you tip the tube up, trap the snake, voilà, job done. There is plenty of reptile behavioural logic behind this approach and it has worked for me a few times with lesser adversaries. My first attempt was met with complete disdain, the second had the snake taking mock stabs at the end of the tube. It appeared this particular snake was unfamiliar with the technique.

I had tried to do the right thing, in a confined space with a lethally venomous creature. It was time to revert to tradition and overcome the competition with superior technology, a perk of being a human rather than, say, a reptile. My weapon of choice was the shotgun, a guaranteed result, but also a guaranteed hole in the bed and side of the tent. The .22 would have to do. It would mostly contain any damage to the snake, if I happened to hit it. So there I was, standing with my upper body leaning into the tent, my lower legs slightly protected by the canvas flap. The sun was angled off my shoulder, unhelpfully shining into the scope.

Things could have been better, unless you support the snake's basic right to life, that is. For its part, the mamba started to shift, probably suspecting that I meant it harm. Half emerged now from beneath the bed, its coffin-shaped head began to rise. Mambas have a very disconcerting ability to hold their upper body high off the ground, all the better for striking at soft targets. I wasn't going to let it reach its chosen height and thus lose my advantage. But the sort of luck that typically deserts you at fairground coconut stalls and clay pigeon shoots didn't fail me.

The mamba was dismayed to find itself shot through the head, its powerful muscles contracting in a death spasm that I expect to one day suffer myself, penance for cruel deeds. Stretched out across the floor of the tent, all one and a half metres of it, it was almost as intimidating in death as alive. Nature makes some creatures perfectly menacing and they suffer for it. If bunny rabbits could inject lethal neurotoxins, we would probably still keep them as childhood pets.

After a close watch to ensure I wasn't going to be pranked by a shamming snake, I moved it out to the kitchen tent as a baboon deterrent. Silvia ventured back into the tent and double checked under the bed for reptilian companions before zipping every opening as tightly as possible. She then got herself on a flight to Victoria Falls for some rest, relaxation and skydiving whilst I played Robinson Crusoe.

The empty camp had become quite an attraction for our more naturally curious neighbours. My first serious intruders arrived later that same day whilst I was out casting flies to disinterested tilapia. As I cut the outboard and drifted into shore, I heard raucous chatter and the unexpected sound of breaking glass. By the time I reached the kitchen tent, all that was left of my antagonists were smashed wine glasses, a few bags of semi-devoured fruit and several fresh turds on the top of the freezers.

The baboons had noticed the camp going quiet, no more pesky humans to chase them off when they ambled too close to the tents. Then they just sat and waited until the single human occupant left for the afternoon. So I had a problem, I couldn't lock the storage tent and I didn't want to have to loiter like some low rent security guard. I was there to expand my horizons, not fend off cheeky monkeys.

I woke the following morning to a familiar racket, the supper club was back. It took an hour to clear up the mess and, whilst I cleaned, I schemed. By the time the last piece of chewed orange peel was swept up, I had devised a plan so simple that even a lone human could handle it.

The troop had a schedule of sorts, foraging early and then again late in the afternoon. I waited patiently for half a day inside the sweltering kitchen. My monkey-logic told me that, if they thought I might always be waiting for them in the tent, they'd stay away. So, I sat in a camp chair, partially hidden by the metal storage racks, and listened as the troop ambled ever closer. It must have been the same for the bananas and apples, listening to their approaching doom.

The older baboons then circled the tent a few times checking for danger and I heard the youngsters scrambling onto the roof to play lookout. Finally, a simian paw appeared under the canvas flap and pulled at the thick velcro strips to create an opening. It was actually fascinating to watch, despite their nefarious intentions. First a snout and then a head appeared as the tomb raider peered inside the tent. He was very relaxed as he expected to find nothing more than free food and a nice place to take a dump.

I didn't want to be in a tent with an entire troop of fanged baboons, but I did let the first three clamber inside, this was my best chance at making a lasting impression. As a safety measure, I'd left a tray of rotting fruit close to the door so they would stay at that end of the large tent. Once they were picking through the delicacies, I jumped to my feet and let them have it with my weapons of choice. A compressed air horn in each hand like a gunslinger. The horns are deafening outside and even better in an enclosed space.

So, fight or flight? The most basic animal instinct. The biggest baboon actually ran through the still zipped entrance, bursting the zip apart on the way. He left a great smear of mango like an exit sign. The other two, Tweedledee and Dumber went through the shade net window which is held in by velcro. They took the entire gauze window section with them as they charged into the bushes. Outside there were primates of all sizes launching themselves from the roof of the tent. Baboons sprinting in all directions, howling and hooting like tormented cavemen.

Inside the tent, all that remained of my three raiders were scattered fruit and three large turds. The shock of the air horns had resulted in an immediate evacuation of baboon bowels. It would be several days before they even came near the camp again, let alone the kitchen tent. Man 1 – Monkey 0.

I sat down with a cigarette to enjoy the approach of sunset and karma prepared to call in her debt. In the safari world, nature and environment sometimes work like some radical human resources department, culling staff at random. I'd toasted a few groups of bemused clients with that darkly hopeful subaltern's mantra, 'Bloody wars and dread diseases!' The voiced aspiration to proceed whilst the competition falters cuts both ways, that dark fortune. It wasn't a snake, an elephant or ebola that ended my exceptional run of luck. It was the admin that finally caught up with me.

I had a track record of sparring with immigration that stretched back almost four years. Shoddy paperwork on my initial application for residency and work permit had become the bane of my working life. The government was in the midst of a vote-winning drive to nationalise as much employment as possible. I completely agreed with the principle, I was just less excited about the practical application when it concerned me personally. I had only just reasserted my dominance over the troop of baboons when the Immigration and Labour Departments managed to gather the correct paperwork to invite me to leave their fine country, with no right of appeal. Happy new millennium!

The fax from Immigration had given me two days to sort my affairs and cross the border. That message had only been read to me in the daily radio check-in three days after its official despatch. I had spent the last month off the radar, idling in a mothballed safari camp. As a result, wrapping up my affairs just involved packing a canvas duffle bag, my fly rod and locking up the booze supplies in camp before I flew into Maun. Despite this monastic simplicity, I did have a bank account which needed to be closed and some pointless paperwork to fill out so that I could return in the future as a standard issue tourist. Silvia had no visa issues at all but needed to get back to her university studies in Austria.

As usual, my own long-term career strategy didn't extend beyond the following week.

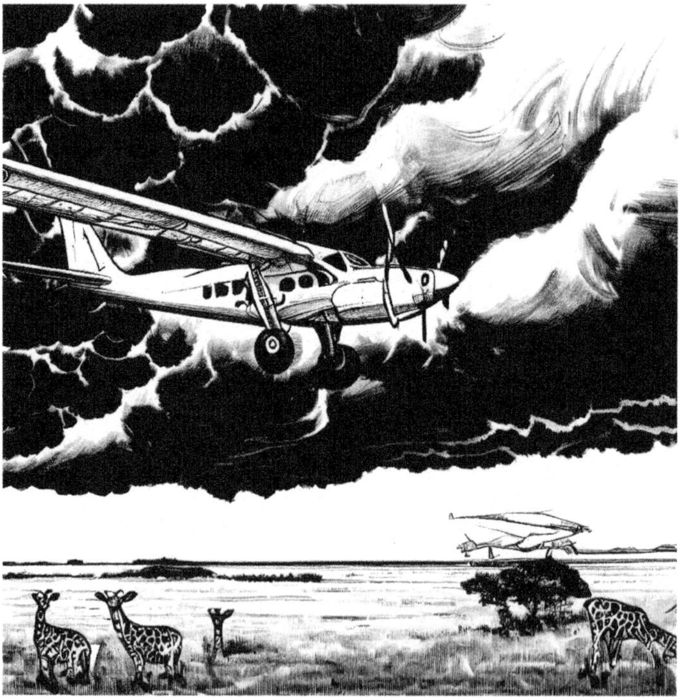

Last Orders at the Bullet and Bush

A mud-spattered Cessna flew us back to Maun, which was in green season tourism mode; relaxing, restocking and drinking heavily before the next onslaught of peak season tourism.

The Immigration Department was on permanent vacation at the best of times and, when I walked through the door, there was a single official propping up the long countertop. I put their fax message down on the counter and, after a cursory glance, was told to return in the morning when the correct official would be on duty. The bank was my only other official duty. After years of enjoying gin and tonic around various campfires, there was just enough capital in my account to be worth a banker's draft.

Unlike the forlorn government offices, the bank was full of customers. I say customers but, on inspection, there were several people asleep on the screwed-down plastic furniture or enjoying a noisy film being played on a wall-mounted television. Only two of the seven manned teller positions were open for business and both of these staff were engrossed in the movie like everyone else. It was a budget kung-fu movie, dubbed and confusing. There was an old man being beaten up by some sort of wizard, who in turn was being pummelled by a younger relative of the old man. They were uprooting trees and flinging them about like Q-tips.

The television was a definite employee perk and had to be more fun than actually doing your job as a high street banker.

There was a long, sluggish queue for the main counter. Fortunately, I didn't have anyone to block my progress to the forex and non-national accounts counter. The only thing missing was an employee of the bank to serve me; the position was open but unmanned. I leant on the counter and scanned the interior of the admin space, hoping to spot a useful staff member. Then I waved at a regular teller, the universal signal for assistance. She waved back with a friendly smile before turning back to the martial arts extravaganza. Finally, a young woman walked over from a row of filing cabinets to explain that she didn't work at the forex counter, but she wanted to be sure I knew she wasn't the person I was looking for.

'Do you know who does work at this counter?'

This seemed a reasonable question.

'No.' She said as she walked back to her files.

A small queue had formed behind me at this point. Anyone standing still for more than five seconds in a bank becomes the head of a queue. This is a global phenomenon; it works in airports, hospital waiting rooms, bus depots. You should try it. My particular queue was watching the film like everyone else. Being in the line served to justify their presence in the bank, which was really just a community cinema.

Unexpectedly, a man approached from behind the counter, making eye contact with me as he walked.

'You can't wait here,' he explained politely.

'Why not?'

'This counter is only for non-nationals and foreign exchange, sir,' he was pretty clear about all of this.

'I am a non-national,' I pointed out.

'Very good sir!' He sat down immediately, 'how may I help you?'

'I want to close my account.'

To this, he handed me a wad of forms and a pen with the bank's logo.

'I'll fill these out somewhere else so you can deal with these other people.' I thumbed over my shoulder at the queue I had started.

'Oh, they are just watching the film, sir,' he smiled happily and joined them as the wizard was buried under a pile of cardboard boulders.

The forms were full of irrelevant questions, every time I queried something, the clerk just told me to skip that section. Finally, I handed back eight pages with my address on the front page and signature on the last, the rest being blank. He happily stamped each page with gusto and said that my bank draft would be ready in the morning.

The day ended at a lodge on the Thamalakane River, mostly locals in sociable huddles and a few off-season tourists in brand new khakis. The night air was pregnant with the promise of more rain, whilst reed frogs and cicadas chorused to each other. Silvia was excited about going back to the mountains, I was less enthusiastic about this sudden change in lifestyle. Lions were more important to me than lederhosen.

The following morning the bank was empty, the television was silent and I recognised the forex clerk behind his counter.

'Good morning!' he called in greeting, 'you are here for your bank draft?'

I was becoming increasingly impressed with this individual. Friendly, efficient, all slightly unexpected after many less successful transactions with major corporations in Botswana.

'Unfortunately, sir, due to a computer error, your draft will not be ready for another two days,' he shrugged apologetically before consulting his desk diary and conceding, 'maybe three days.'

'Unfortunately,' I exclaimed, 'I am flying out of your country this afternoon.'

'Ah, that is doubly unfortunate!' he smiled contentedly, glancing behind me to check if there were other customers he might help.

'Is there anything you can do to speed this up?'

I knew that there wouldn't be, but we are all optimists, aren't we?

'I regret that we are at the mercy of our computer system,' he indicated a time-worn desktop PC nearby, a visual representation of the tired condition of his employer's software.

'On behalf of the bank, I can guarantee the readiness of your draft in two or three days sir!'

He was a pretty convincing liar.

In Austria, you would probably insist on seeing the manager and getting the service you expect there and then. In Maun, I figured this was the service that I expected. I now had to get an extension on my rejected visa to avoid being arrested at the airport. It was proving almost as hard to leave Botswana legally as it had been to live there legally.

It was ten o'clock by the time I reached the cluster of cement buildings that made up the Immigration Department. The national flag hung limp as pond weed in the oppressive humidity of early January. Like the bank, the offices were almost empty of customers and a lone official sat behind the counter. She was idly drawing symmetrical patterns on the back of someone's visa application and didn't look up as I walked in.

'Can I help you?' she said to her artwork. It wasn't phrased as a question, more like a statement, like *will* I help you.

'I need to get an extension on my visa,' I spoke to the top of her head, 'two...three days until the bank can provide a draft and close my account.'

'Please remove your hat,' was the reply, still directed at the desk.

'I'm sorry?'

'You can't wear a hat inside a government office, it is disrespectful to the president.'

She finally looked up, bloodshot eyes, her mouth set in a slight frown, an emotional stonewall.

There is something negatively transformative about employment in low level bureaucracy where gatekeepers can become very hostile. Perhaps they feel the weight of responsibility, keeping the flotsam and jetsam of the species out of their territories? Low salaries and mind numbingly repetitive tasks probably don't increase their chances of developing into charming humans either.

'That guy is wearing a hat,' I stupidly pointed out her colleague, slouched in an office chair with his green beret in place.

'He is wearing the correct uniform.'

This was delivered without any attempt at concealing her annoyance. I was going to suggest that really she should be wearing a hat as well then, but I managed to stop myself as I removed my own hat in a conciliatory gesture. I felt we had already started our relationship badly and, in truth, she held all the cards.

'You can close your account from outside Botswana,' she stated, 'why do you need an extension?'

She had a point. In theory, I could try to get a bank in Europe to communicate with my bank in Maun, but I knew that would come up snake eyes. Most African presidents take their cash with them whenever they leave the country, even on short working trips as sensible asset management.

'It is company policy,' I pointed at the faded logo on my shirt, 'something to do with accounting and Botswana tax law.' I was lying as smoothly as my friend at the bank.

'If I have to leave today, I'll need to produce a letter from your department to explain why I didn't follow the standard procedure.'

The angry canvas dented with a deeper frown, extra paperwork is the least entertaining part of this game.

'I would be truly grateful if you could help me out.'

This must be how people trapped in abusive relationships feel.

'You must present a letter from your employer explaining these facts.'

She leaned back, the ball in my court for a moment.

'No problem, what time do you close for lunch?'

The clock on the wall said it was quarter past eleven.

'We are closed from twelve until two and then we shut at three as it is a Tuesday.'

Tuesday it seemed, was national slackers' day.

The letter was easy. I went back to company HQ and typed up some nonsense on nice letterhead paper. Lots of sham-legalise and mock-Latin, then had my boss sign the thing. He was glum to be losing a management team out of the blue. I was sorry to be losing my superb camp in the Savuti channel and to be thrown out of the country like some migrant worker, which is exactly what I was.

Though the altered state that I chose to live in had nothing at all to do with draining the local economy to my own benefit, my bank account was proof of that. I was part of a small class of migrants, a lifestyle refugee. An economic migrant wants better employment and earning opportunities, something they lack at home. A lifestyle refugee wants a way of life denied them in their own country; the wages were irrelevant as long as I had the life. Why else would a degree educated European submit

Shambolic

himself to this shambolic existence? Simple, it was entertaining beyond comparison. I suspect my adversaries at the Immigration Department wouldn't have thought much of this explanation.

I now had the required document in my back pocket and a few hours to kill which gave me time to change my ticket for the afternoon flight to Johannesburg. A flight that I wouldn't be on. Air Botswana had a cunningly located office, well away from the airport to prevent disgruntled clients from harassing airline staff. The flimsy pre-fab buildings look something like take-away food containers. Actually, they smell a bit like them as well. I was surprised that the door was open when I arrived as it was close to midday and that usually signals a down tools in Maun. The single staff member was eating a towering sandwich at his desk and wasn't especially pleased to see a customer wander in.

'Flight enquiries and timetables are available at the airport,' he tried to head me off at the pass.

'I need to get the date changed on my ticket.'

'Oh.' He looked sad and put his sandwich down. I put my ticket on the desk for his inspection and explained the extra time I would need in Maun.

'Our computer system isn't working today,' he said as he read the ticket, 'so I can't alter your ticket at the moment.'

It seemed everyone in town was using the same computer or the same excuse.

'So what happens in two days when I try to use this ticket?'

It was a reasonable question from a paying customer.

'Just tell them at the airport that the computer was broken.'

He made it sound so ridiculously obvious that only a fool would ask. His right hand slowly pulled the sandwich back into the centre of the desk.

'Can you write a note explaining that for the check-in staff?'

Fail to prepare and you prepare to fail and so on.

His left hand reached over to a pile of photocopied sheets and handed me the top copy. It was a faded, over-copied document that read; *'Through no fault of are own; the computer system at Air Botswana is no functioning:::Pleese extend all curtsey to these most valued customer. Think you.'*

Before I could engage in further discussion, the Dagwood was jammed firmly back into his mouth with a shrug that translated as, 'Sorry, I am eating a sandwich now and cannot answer any further questions!'

I heard the door lock behind me as I left.

Although I should have been tired of traipsing around town by now, I was finding the Sisyphean task to be something of a distraction from the bleak reality of a return to Europe mid-winter.

The Immigration offices were open as promised at two o'clock and the hat fetishist was at her post. I delivered the letter, which was immediately discarded to one side, and watched as various papers were shuffled in a final demonstration of authority. My passport was scrutinised once again and, finally, the officer picked up her heavy rubber stamp. The date was changed, slowly, on the rolling mechanism, fresh ink applied, time itself seemed to stagnate. Then the desk 'phone rang and that small plastic tool, carrying the full weight of the Botswana government behind it, was set back onto the ink blotter. The telephone call involved a lot of giggling and cord twisting, it didn't appear to be official business. The beret-wearing junior colleague was listening in and shrugged at me in silent solidarity. Clearly the rubber stamp wasn't his responsibility. Eventually, the call ended and the stamp was once again raised. I waited, the beret waited and the stamp came down with such violence that he jumped in his chair. The woman and I both stared at the passport for a second before I grabbed it, just in case she decided to erase the bright red print using some establishment hex.

The room was absolutely silent aside from the whirring of the ceiling fan and then the door opened behind me. The spell was broken by a sunburned American.

'I lost my passport,' he said, 'the police said I should report it here.'

'We close the department at three,' a challenge from behind the counter, rather than a citizens' advice announcement.

Everyone, including the office junior, looked at the wall clock, which said quarter past two. I opened the door and didn't look back.

The heat was more intense in the courtyard now, a muddy square of hard-packed earth bordered with neat flowerbeds. The afternoon rain threatened but didn't deliver for the next couple of days. I passed the time discussing alternatives to my life in the Okavango with friends. The safari business soaks into all of the remotest wilderness in Africa. It is like a flash flood of opportunity and potential in an economic desert. Namibia, named for the great dune sea, was mentioned as a possible continuation of this experiential grand tour.

Whilst the bank dithered and then delivered the crucial banker's draft, a pilot friend offered us a ride to South Africa. He was taking an aircraft down for servicing and then moving on to a new job in Hong Kong. Our final few hours in Botswana were spent in a bar overlooking the busy airstrip. It used to be the flyers' drinking hole but had been bought by a South African pub chain, the Bull and Bush. It was most famous for a drunken shooting on opening night. Maun's drinking society hadn't wasted the golden opportunity to rechristen the place the *Bullet and Bush*.

From my bar stool, I could see the luggage being offloaded from an inbound Cape Town flight and then back onto the trailer for the outbound Johannesburg flight. There were going to be some grumpy tourists at the luggage carousel. Consigned to a week of wearing badly fitting curio shop T-shirts on safari, nothing says 'lost luggage' louder than a middle-aged man in an XXL T-shirt with a laughing cartoon hippo on the front.

The wall clock in the bar eventually ticked around to midday, last orders for the soon-to-be-deported. My pilot friend ran his pre-flight checks, then we sat and waited in the shade of the wing for half an hour due to a flight plan mix-up. He was distracted by a bad stomach and the stress of a move overseas. Overhead the summer rain clouds converged to a shroud of heavy grey without end and the heat, trapped, became oppressive. The tower finally waved us into action. Our pilot fired up the engine and we were engulfed in that familiar frame vibration from a turbo prop that makes it hard to stay awake. One final thumbs up from our pilot before he turned back to pour on some throttle and, suddenly, we were wheels up, no longer physically connected to Botswana.

Maun, full of donkeys and friends, receded into the rear view as the horizon was filled with the Kalahari. After the evergreen Okavango, it felt like flying into nothing. The pilot's weather report said that Gauteng and environs had been hammered with rain for a week. This weather would blow its way north and eventually leave thousands flooded from their homes in northern Botswana. I drifted in and out of sleep, lulled by the mesmeric vibration of the airframe. We entered South African airspace on autopilot.

It was very peaceful in the cabin as it finally started to rain.

Epilogue

Less than a year later, I would find myself back in Africa, guiding clients on Namibia's Skeleton Coast. The desert forced a complete recalibration of what defined wilderness. It would be difficult to find a more contrasting environment to the lush wetlands of Botswana. Towering sand dunes crumbling into the cold Atlantic surf. Bleached whale bones and rusted shipwrecks dotting the shore like grave markers in the eerie morning fog. The vast scale of the landscape dwarfing my tiny safari outpost.

Despite the alien habitat, there were still welcome familiarities. The wildlife could be frustratingly elusive, especially the scattered herds of desert-adapted elephants. Who knew a 6,000 kg male elephant could be a master at hide and seek? Namibia's precious black rhino population were ill-tempered characters who enjoyed targeting anyone dumb enough to walk into their personal space. Snakes still ambushed my guests in their tents and scorpions haunted their shoes. An inventive thief made off with the camp safe. Then, once a year, nature would gather her fury to wash our flimsy tented camps from the face of the earth with seasonal floods.

It was good to be back.

Glossary

Bakkie: pickup truck
Batswana (plural) / Motswana (singular): dominant ethnic group of Botswana
Bliksem: bastard! (Afrikaans)
Bru: slang for dude
Bunny chow: Indian fast food
Bush TV: campfire
Camp manager: actually the most important person in a safari camp (thinks guides are a cost liability)
CITES: Convention on International Trade in Endangered Species of Wild Fauna and Flora
Coaster: slang for beyond cool
Dumatau: safari camp on the Botswana/Namibia border
Eish: multi-purpose proclamation of dismay or shock
Howzit: casual greeting 'How is it?'
Igundane: rat (isiZulu)
Indlamu: traditional Zulu dance (isiZulu)
Jao: island village in the North West Okavango Delta
Jedibe Island Camp: closest safari camp to Jao village, now closed
Just now: slang for impending action, not necessarily immediate
Kief: slang for cool (Arabic)
Kwena: crocodile (Setswana)
Kubu: hippo (Setswana)
Land Rover Series III: pre-modern conveyance which runs on luck
Lapa: courtyard or enclosure
Lata: thin wooden poles used for decorative construction
Lekker: great/nice (Afrikaans)
Matata: a problem (Setswana)
Maun: donkey sanctuary in Northern Botswana
Mieliepap: maize porridge (Afrikaans)
Moeder: mother (Afrikaans)
Mokoro: traditional dugout canoe (mekoro – plural) (Setswana)
Monnas: men (Setswana)

Ngashi: pole for propelling mokoro (Setswana)
Now now: slang for *almost* immediate action
Ntondo: male reproductive organ (Setswana)
Okavango Delta: a UNESCO protected 'inland delta' in North West Botswana
Overlander: low-cost truck safari
Rra: Sir/Mr (Setswana)
Safari guide: the most important person in a safari camp (thinks managers are superfluous)
Sangoma: traditional healer (isiZulu)
Savuti Bush Camp: safari camp on the Savuti Channel
Seronga: riverside village in the Okavango panhandle
Stoep: verandah (Afrikaans)
Takkie: sports shoe (Afrikaans)
Tsamaya sentle: go well (Setswana)
ZCC: Zionist Christian Church

Printed in Great Britain
by Amazon